D1252407

TRAILERABLE SAILBOATS

Books by Christopher Caswell

Championship Dinghy Sailing (with David Ullman)
Trailerable Sailboats

TRAILERABLE SAILBOATS

Christopher Caswell

**PHOTOGRAPHS AND DRAWINGS
BY THE AUTHOR**

W·W·NORTON & COMPANY

NEW YORK   LONDON

Library of Congress Cataloging in Publication Data

Caswell, Christopher.
Trailerable sailboats.

Includes index.
1. Sailboats. I. Title.
VM351.C34   1982   623.8'223   81–18983
ISBN 0–393–03271–X   AACR2

W. W. Norton & Company, Inc. 500 Fifth Avenue, New York, N.Y. 10110
W. W. Norton & Company Ltd. 37 Great Russell Street, London WC1B 3NU

This book is dedicated to my parents, Peggy and Jack, who introduced me to the world of sailing, and to my wife, Beth, who now shares my enthusiasm for it.

Contents

Foreword   *9*

Why Buy a Trailerable Sailboat?   *11*

Acknowledgments

SECTION I   Buying the Trailerable Sailboat

1. *Making the Basic Decisions*   19
2. *How to Start Looking*   23
3. *What to Look For in a New Trailerable Sailboat*   28
    SAILING ABILITY   28
    INTERIOR LAYOUT   32
    CONSTRUCTION   38
    STORAGE SPACE   55
    PRICE   59
    THE BUILDER   62
4. *What to Order with the New Boat*   64
5. *What to Look For in a Used Boat*   76
    THE YACHT BROKER AND HOW TO USE HIM   80
    THE SURVEYOR AND WHAT HE CAN SAVE YOU   82
6. *Commissioning Your Boat Properly*   86

SECTION II   Outfitting the Trailerable Sailboat

7. *Sails and Covers*   91
8. *Engines*   97
9. *Galley Gear*   103

10. *Electronics*   111
11. *Safety Equipment*   119

SECTION III   The Trailer

12. *Buying Tips*   127
13. *The Tow Car*   132
14. *Trailer Hitches*   135
15. *Towing*   137

SECTION IV   Living with the Trailerable Sailboat

16. *Launching and Retrieving*   143
17. *Boat Handling*   146
18. *Seamanship*   153
19. *Emergencies*   160
20. *Storage*   165
21. *Navigation*   169
22. *Cruising*   173
23. *Racing*   177
24. *Legal Affairs*   189

SECTION V   Maintenance

25. *Hull, Deck, and Interior*   197
26. *Spars, Rigging, and Sails*   203
27. *Engine*   207
28. *Trailer*   209

Appendices   211
    I. Trailer Boat Clubs   211
    II. Tools   212
    III. Spare Parts   213
    IV. First-Aid Supplies   214

Index   215

Foreword

Pick any weekend and drop by your local launching ramp. You're liable to see many sailboats, once considered too big to be trailered, now waiting in line to launch for a weekend of sailing.

To say that the trailerable sailboat is the hottest new trend in sailing is an understatement. Dozens of builders are churning out thousands of new trailerable sailboats every year. This book is dedicated to those boats and the people who buy them.

It isn't a comprehensive book, by any means—you'd need an encyclopedia for that. But it is directed specifically at the trailerable sailboat, those boats of 20 to 30 feet that can be comfortably handled by the average family.

Too many books attempt to cover the entire sailing field from tiny dinghies to huge ocean racers, and they end up doing nothing well. This book won't teach you how to sail—there are excellent books for that. Nor will it explain the racing rules or brief you on how to predict the weather. It doesn't even have two hundred boating recipes.

What this book does have is a lot of information on how to choose, purchase, outfit, and live with one specific boat: the trailerable sailboat. It's full of the nitty-gritty, those details, applicable only to these boats, that are overlooked or glossed over in other books.

Welcome to the world of the trailerable sailboat!

Christopher Caswell

November 1981

Why Buy a Trailerable Sailboat?

There are several reasons to buy a trailerable sailboat. But which ones are important enough to convince you depends on you. For example, a rich but inexperienced sailor might not worry about cost savings, while an experienced but poor sailor might not be concerned about the ease of handling in these boats. So the reasons are offered in no particular order, and you can choose any or all for your own purposes.

GO ANYWHERE. A trailerable sailboat can go almost anywhere. If the tow vehicle can reach the water's edge, then you have a new cruising ground. Once in the water, a trailerable sailboat can explore shallow areas that larger yachts must avoid for fear of running aground. Yet the trailerable boat can handle deep water just like bigger vessels.

With no home port, you can venture far from your own local waters. In fact, that's what most trailerable sailboat owners do. The average large yacht rarely cruises more than 50 to 75 miles from its home mooring simply because of the pressures of time on the skipper. It takes days to sail more than a few hundred miles. But the trailerable sailboat, cruising down the freeway at 55 mph, can cover great distances in short time spans. And wouldn't you really rather spend your time at the cruise destination than in getting there?

If you draw a circle around your home city at a distance of 150 to 250 miles, you'll find enough rivers, lakes, harbors, and coves to satisfy

If the tow car can get to the water's edge, then the trailerable sailboat can explore a new area, as in this shot of Lake Pleasant in Arizona.

a year of cruising without duplicating yourself. And that distance can be covered with a trailerable sailboat on a Friday afternoon, leaving the weekend free for exploration and loafing.

EASY TO STORE. In the good old days of boat buying, you simply went down to the local harbor, asked the dockmaster for a slip, and put your boat in it upon delivery. Unfortunately, those days are long gone in most parts of the country. The waiting list for slips in some areas, Southern California and Florida in particular, can be as long as twelve years for 20- to 30-foot boats! Along with this wait is the cost of keeping a boat in the water. The average slip rent in 1980 was about $4 per foot of boat per month, or $80 per month for a 20-footer. In certain popular boating areas, rents can range as high as $8 per foot!

But with a trailerable sailboat, you don't have to worry about renting a slip. Your trailer is your mooring, and you can park it anywhere—in your own driveway, in your backyard, in the garage, or in one of the many recreation-vehicle storage lots springing up across the country. The cost? Anywhere from nothing for the use of your own yard to a nominal fee for a storage yard.

EASY TO HANDLE. The difficulty of handling any boat increases dramatically with the size of the boat. And the effort needed to operate the boat increases at the same rate. While your daughter can handle the jib on a 20-foot trailerable sailboat without much difficulty, she wouldn't even be able to budge the sails on a 40-footer without help from your football-letterman son. If you want to slip away from a long week at work, you can go by yourself on a summer evening in a 20-footer. But you'll get little relaxation trying to singlehand a 40-footer.

Along with this size/difficulty formula is a similar size/problem ratio. Problems on small boats tend to remain small problems, while problems on a big boat can get out of hand quickly. No matter how experienced the yachtsman, we all make mistakes. Underestimating how fast you're going when docking a big boat can cause thousands of dollars in damage, but the same mistake in a 20-foot trailerable will probably only result in your embarrassment.

LESS UPKEEP. Maintenance for a trailerable sailboat just means a washdown after a weekend of sailing. Once or twice a year, it's a good idea to apply a coat of wax to protect the fiberglass and restore its shine, but that's a project for a sunny afternoon. If you have woodwork, you'll need to renew the varnish occasionally, the sails will need hosing off to remove salt and dirt, and a vacuum cleaner will take care of the interior. But that's about it. You don't have to paint the bottom every year with antifouling paint to prevent barnacles unless you leave the boat in the water for long periods, you don't have to schedule a yearly haul-out for paint and underwater maintenance, and you don't have to worry about your yacht when a storm roars through the local harbor.

If you need to make major repairs, it's always less expensive when you can simply drive the boat to your repairman and leave it. With a waterbound yacht, you must either haul out at a shipyard (more money) or pay the travel time for a repairmen to call on the boat at its slip.

SAVE MONEY. In an age of inflation, it's always nice to save money where you can. A trailer boat is almost always less expensive than a similarly sized craft designed to stay in the water year round. And this isn't because a trailerable is cheaply built. Rather, it's a function of the basic design. A full-keel yacht needs a ton or more of lead to stay upright, and the hull is deeper and fatter than a trailerable. Those differences mean money. A trailerable sailboat, with its shallow hull and swinging keel, requires less fiberglass, less lead for the keel, and there are additional savings from a production line set up to build many trailerables rather than just a few keel boats. And since fiberglass is a petrochemical, the energy crisis is only going to raise the cost of every pound of fiberglass used in your boat. You're better off buying a 5,000-pound boat than a 12,000-pound boat.

SMALL, BUT BIG ENOUGH. Last but not least, a trailerable sailboat is small enough for some things, but big enough for others. Sure, there are some drawbacks to its size, but overall, a trailerable sailboat is a pretty efficient little craft.

It's small enough so that you can singlehand it yourself, yet the cockpit can hold several adults comfortably· on a cruise. It's small enough to be trailerable (and that means a beam of 8 feet in most areas), but it's big enough for deep-sea sailing. Most experienced sailors agree that it is rarely the vessel that fails in a crisis, but rather the crew. A trailerable sailboat can ride out a storm at sea just like a larger vessel, and, in some sea conditions, you might even be better off with a light-weight boat than with a heavy displacement yacht.

I don't want to be at sea in a severe storm in a trailerable boat any more than I want to be there in any vessel. But, given good seamanship and safe boat handling, the trailerable is just as safe as the larger yacht.

As mentioned before, the shallow draft of the trailerable allows explorations of coves and lakes that would be dangerous for deeper or bigger yachts. And because a trailerable sailboat is lightweight, running aground isn't a disaster—it's simply a delay until you push yourself off.

Inside, you shouldn't expect the luxury and space of a 40-footer. On the other hand, you'll find all the comforts of home (and perhaps some that you don't have at home). Full-length bunks will sleep a family of four comfortably on most trailerables, and the galley can whip up a hot meal better than most highway restaurants serve.

There's fresh air, exercise, healthy appetites, new surroundings, and

One of the recognizable features of most trailerable sailboats is the swing keel, shown here in profile on a Catalina-22. When fully extended downward, it provides stability and control equal to a sailboat with a normal keel. But in the retracted position (dotted line), it allows the boat to explore shallow waters and fit on a low trailer.

excitement to be found in sailing a trailerable. A warm summer breeze makes for an afternoon run to a new cove, where the stillness surrounds you as you tuck in for the night. With the dawn comes another day on the water in your own yacht and more coves to explore. As the Water Rat said in *Wind in the Willows,* "There is nothing, absolutely nothing, half so much worth doing as simply messing about in boats."

~~~~~~~~~~~~~~~~~~~~~~~~~~~~~~~~~

Buying the Trailerable Sailboat

1

Making the Basic Decisions

Next to buying a home, a boat is probably the biggest investment you'll make in your life. And since a boat is going to cost about what a house did just a few years ago, put your efforts into making a wise choice. You'll never regret it.

In today's highly competitive market, your chances of buying a badly built boat are less than they have ever been, although some caution is still required. But most dealers and yacht brokers note that the biggest mistake made by first-time boat buyers is that they buy the "wrong" boat.

What is a "wrong" boat? It's one that doesn't fit the needs of that particular buyer. It may be too big or too small, it may be too fast or too slow, it may be intended for purposes other than what the buyer plans to use it for. To avoid the problem of having the wrong boat, make some basic decisions before you walk into the showroom.

First, what can you afford? All of the following questions require honest answers, but none so much as this one. How much money do you feel you can spend at this time on a boat? You'll need to include not only the base price of the boat, but all the other items that will crop up each year: maintenance, repairs, storage, insurance and registration, and so forth. Once you've settled on a dollar figure, stick to it and don't allow yourself to be inched upward by a glib salesman: "After all, it's only a couple of thousand dollars more!"

When you make your financial assessment, you should probably check with a local bank for at least a general dollar figure on financing. After you decide on a particular boat, you can start shopping around various banking institutions for the best loan. But these rates change almost daily, and right now you just want a ball-park number. Let's say you can spend, in cash, $6,000 this year. If the finance payments on a $15,000 boat, including down payment, will come to $5000, then you're going to be in the ballpark.

The biggest financial mistake you can make is to purchase a boat that sells for $9,999 when you have an honest $10,000 budget. You won't be able to afford insurance, trailer registration, extras for the boat, or repairs for any accidents. Buy a boat that leaves you a comfortable cushion in your boat budget for all those things you never knew you needed. And don't let anyone kid you: there is absolutely no such thing as a boat "ready to sail away." You may get it away from the dock and it may have cushions and anchors and various accessories, but what about pots and pans for the galley, a dinghy, blankets or sleeping bags for the bunks, a clock, or any of a multitude of items you'll want to have. Once you've been realistic about what you can spend, don't automatically assume you *have* to spend it all.

The next question to ask yourself is what you plan to do with your boat. You probably aren't a racing enthusiast yet. But if you're highly competitive in other ways, you may find that racing is for you. On the other hand, your boat may become a getaway from the business week, and your pleasures will be cruising to a quiet cove and contemplating your toes while you sprawl in the cockpit. Perhaps you have no enthusiasm for spending the night aboard, and you simply want to take family and friends for afternoon sails around the harbor. Each of those three categories would send you in a vastly different direction in your hunt for a boat. The day sailor is going to want a nice big cockpit with marginal amenities in the cabin, while the overnighter wants more cabin space. The racer will be willing to give up creature comforts in the cockpit and cabin if he or she can find a boat slightly faster than anyone else's.

Once you've decided on the first two questions, all the other considerations should fall into place as a result. You should start thinking about how big a boat you want. Don't forget that you can buy a boat that is too big just as easily as you can buy one that is too small. You'll need to review your plans and establish an idea of how many people you'll have for crew. A big boat, even a 30-footer, can be a handful if you're alone or you're the only one aboard who knows how to sail. On the other hand, if you plan to take your family of six every weekend, you'd better have enough space so they don't leave you with the boat while they take up roller skating.

Since we're talking strictly about trailerable sailboats and because you'll certainly end up towing your boat at least to and from the launch ramp, give some thought to your car. Don't plan to pull a 3-ton boat behind a Volkswagen. If you happen to have a VW, you should include the cost of a more powerful tow car in your budget figures.

Where are you going to keep your boat? You'll have a trailer, but if you only have space for a 23-foot boat in your backyard, you probably won't be entirely happy with a 25-footer. If you plan to store it at a local RV storage yard, check with them to see what their maximum size limits are.

Are you a fanatic about owning only new products? If so, you'll probably limit your search to dealerships with new boats. If, on the other hand, you're willing to put up with someone else's scratches and nicks, you can save some money by looking at used boats.

Where are you going to use your boat? Consider the normal weather conditions such as wind and waves, the depth of the water, and any other factors in your local area. A sailboat with tall masts and an expanse of sail area is probably just right for Long Island Sound, where the winds are generally light, but that same boat will make you miserable in the daily gusts of San Francisco Bay. So check the local conditions, and narrow your search to a boat that will be suitable for that area.

What kind of boat do you like? That may seem a foolish question at this stage, but it's really not. If you have any interest at all in boats, then you've already seen some that you thought were good looking. You'll be a lot happier in the long run with a boat that appeals to you than with one that strikes you as ugly every time you see it. If you like classic looks, there are some trailerable sailboats that imitate vintage sailboats.

Some people dislike the flush-deck style while others like it. It's one of preference, but don't be embarrassed to skip over one boat simply because you don't like its looks. That just makes you one of millions of boating enthusiasts. After all, you wouldn't buy an ugly car or an ugly house. Why buy an ugly boat?

2

~~~~~~~

How to Start Looking

By now you'll have made the basic decisions and you can start your search for the right trailerable sailboat. But where do you start?

There is, to my knowledge, no local newspaper or urban newspaper that does not have a classified section full of boat ads. It's a fact of life that there are boats everywhere. You can start by looking through the ads, many of which are placed by local dealers. You'll be able to see which dealers handle trailerable sailboats.

At the same time, start buying the boating magazines (if you haven't already) and read the ads with care. Several national and all of the local boating magazines have extensive brokerage advertising that can give you some idea of prices on various designs. When you're studying the prices, don't forget that location can make a difference in price. For example, a boat built in Newport Beach is less expensive to buy there than it is in Florida simply because of the cost of transportation. So use the ads in your area.

Make use of the "bingo" cards in the boating magazines. By circling the numbers of ads that interest you, you can start the process of collecting brochures without the strain of fighting off a salesman . . . yet.

Sooner or later you're going to have to make the rounds of the showrooms. Pick up all the literature you can find on boats in your size

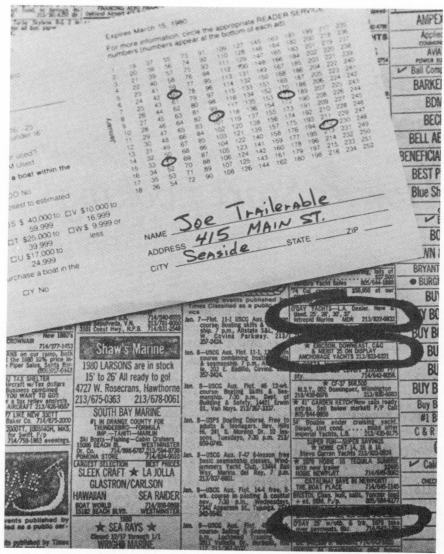

Two good ways to get information about trailerables are the newspaper classified ads and the bingo card from boating magazines.

and price range, climb through as many boats in the showroom as possible, and perhaps arrange for demonstration sails. You may not have a clear idea of what to look for on a demonstration yet, but the sail itself may help make some of your decisions. Besides, as you focus on a particular boat, the dealer will be happy to take you out again, especially when he senses that you're serious.

An all-sailboat show is a good way to start your shopping for a new boat, since you can compare the various models side by side in one place. Don't forget to look at equipment that you might want as well.

After you've studied the newspapers and the magazines and toured the showrooms, what more can you do? Plenty.

Along with the boating boom has come a boat-show boom, and you will probably find that there are several near you. No longer are boat shows held only in January and February to première the new season; now there are spring boat shows and fall boat shows and midsummer boat shows. In addition, you may find an in-the-water boat show nearby, where the boats are afloat and accessible.

Perhaps the advice to keep your eyes open at a boat show is foolish, because you'll be wide-eyed at the acres of shiny fiberglass and dacron. But try to get aboard every boat in your size range so that you'll have as wide a scope of comparison as possible. At the same time, don't neglect the exhibits of equipment and hardware. You might even start picking up brochures on items you think you may want, like radios or outboard motors, so that you can discuss them intelligently when you negotiate for your boat.

An example of a special offer made to buyers at a boat show. With a reputable dealer, you should be able to get the same deal shortly after the boat show as well.

One world of caution. Don't be misled into buying a boat at a boat show simply because there is a "boat-show special price." This is simply a promotional offer from the local dealer, and you can, with any reputable company, walk into the showroom a week after the boat show and get the same price.

What else can you do to help make your boat-buying decision? Broaden your horizons, for starters. Skip mowing the lawn on Saturday morning (it'll get used to it anyway) and head for the nearby launching ramp. You'll see a lot of different styles being launched, and you can get some idea of what kind of boats are popular in your area. If a particular brand is especially prominent, it may be that the local dealer is energetic, that the prices are inviting, or that the boat has characteristics suitable to the area. For whatever reason, you should investigate further.

Boating people are perhaps the friendliest group to be found in any sport. So don't hesitate to ask a question of a trailerable-sailboat owner. He'll probably talk your ear off, and you may even wangle an invitation for a future sail. A word of caution, though: try to ask your question when the time is appropriate. Don't ask about his boat as he tries to back the trailer into the water or as he is lifting the mast into place.

If your local waterways have a sailing club (and most do), stop by and check out the offerings on their bulletin board. You may find just the boat you want before it's been advertised in the newspapers. And you might also find some skippers who are looking for crews, another way to get experience on a particular boat.

Last, this is a good time to enroll in a basic boating course. Both the United States Power Squadron and the United States Coast Guard Auxiliary host free boating classes year around, and you can't go wrong. The classes cover the basics of seamanship, navigation,and boat handling. After passing the basic course, you can continue in advanced studies, such as sailing, if you wish. The knowledge is valuable, and you'll have the chance to meet boating people in your own area.

3

~~~~~~

What to Look For in a New Trailerable Sailboat

Sailing Ability

Now we come to a knotty problem. Without knowing how to sail, as most first timers don't, judging the sailing quality of a boat is like buying an airplane without a pilot's license. Until you acquire more firsthand knowledge, you're going to have to rely on some outside sources as well as your common sense.

At this point, you're starting to narrow your boat quest to several different models. Use all your guile to find out the truth about each boat. Contact owners shamelessly when you see them aboard, or leave notes on their boats and ask them to call you. You'll get a good reading on how well the boat performs, and you may hear some good or bad tales about how the boat is built or sold.

You may have a friend with sailing experience. If possible, have him accompany you on your demonstration sails, but don't rely solely on his judgment. He may have certain interests or prejudices that don't match with your own needs.

Read everything you can about the boat in question. Ask the dealer if he can supply you with boat test reports from national magazines, and track down any comments made by other magazines.

There are a few things you can check, regardless of your own sailing abilities. First, make inquiries about the stability of the boat. As the old Packard ads used to say, "Ask the man who owns one." Find out if there are any sailing problems with the boat that might conflict with your own plans.

Don't buy a boat that doesn't have self-righting abilities. This simply means that if a gust of wind hits you hard enough to knock the boat far onto its side, it will return to its normal upright stance. The weight of the keel/centerboard, the shape of the hull, and the size of the mast and sails will all affect this righting ability.

In the Midget Ocean Racing Fleet, which administers racing in small boats like trailerables, self-righting is actually tested by pulling the boat over on its side until the mast is horizontal, and then tying the sailbags onto the mast. When released, the boat has to snap upright or it won't be allowed to race. This type of test also shows whether water can find its way into the boat in a drastic "knockdown". Don't expect to need self-righting in your everyday afternoon sail, but it is a good indication of design integrity and overall seaworthiness of the boat.

Most sailboats spend their time at a heel angle of less than 25°, which is normal. If, on your demonstration sail, you find the boat continually heeled far over with the lee side underwater, you're probably sailing aboard a boat that has insufficient ballast or too much sail area. If the day is particularly windy, you can write it off to the skipper using too much sail. But if the day seems normal, you should check with other owners to see if this boat has a problem with stability.

For the more experienced sailor, there are several ways to check the basic sailing ability of a boat. First, there is the "feel" of the boat under sail. A well-designed and well-tuned sailboat should balance, which means that there will be a little pull one way or the other on the tiller. This constant pressure, especially when the boat is sailing close-hauled, is called "helm." There are two kinds: weather helm will turn the boat into the wind if the tiller is released; lee helm will turn the boat away from the wind. Lee helm is an absolute indicator that something is wrong: either the boat is badly designed or badly tuned. Allowing the mast to lean aft may cure lee helm, but the matter should be investigated before you purchase a similar boat. Weather helm is often tuned "into" an otherwise neutral sailboat so that the skipper will be able to feel the helm. Weather helm is also a safety valve, since a big gust will cause the boat to turn upwind and spill air from the sails or, if the skipper falls overboard, the boat will turn into the wind and stop.

Beyond this simple test for helm, there is also an overall feel to a boat. There should be a solidity to it as it goes over and through waves that you may not find on an extremely lightweight boat or one that is poorly designed. If the bow and stern have long overhangs, the boat will tend to hobbyhorse, or rock up and down in small waves. The current design trend is toward short overhangs, which eliminate the problem, but keep the concept in mind.

It's very difficult to measure how close to the wind a sailboat can actually sail, and the difference between a very good sailboat and a very bad sailboat will only be a few degrees at most. But most modern sailboats should be able to tack through an angle of 45° before going head to wind. Even a novice can check this on the compass during a demonstration sail with a competent skipper. When the boat is sailing close-hauled, make a mental note of the compass course. After the boat tacks and has settled down, check the compass again. It should indicate a difference of about 90° from the last course. That means you went 45° into the wind and then another 45° to fill the sails on the new tack.

During the sailing demonstration, you'll get a good idea of how easy the boat is to rig and sail. See if the cockpit is large enough to handle your planned guests and crew, and decide whether the necessary winches and sailing hardware are placed for convenient use.

Don't be afraid to get up and walk around during the sail, and see what the cabin is like while the boat is under sail. If possible, set part of the demonstration time aside for powering so that you can see how the boat responds under power, and how difficult it is to rig the outboard for use.

This trailerable sailboat has a considerable amount of weather helm, as evidenced by the helmsman holding the tiller to windward while steering a straight course. A little weather helm is good to have, but this much indicates a design problem or too much sail area.

Interior Layout

Layout is the sailing term for the formula that allows you to fit people, food, bunks, clothing, sails, toilet, kitchen, and sailing gear into a space about the size of your family car. It isn't impossible, but there are some things you have to give up and there are some things you should watch out for.

Cabin fever is the maritime version of that feeling you get after you've had a cold for a week: you just can't stand to stay inside for one more minute! To prevent cabin fever and to sandwich all those items into the cabin of a trailerable sailboat requires two good people: you and the designer.

Let's start with the designer, because you have to decide whether you like his solutions or not. In trailerable sailboats there is one basic interior arrangement, and all others are simply variations of this. Starting at the bow, there is a pair of V berths followed by a pair of settee berths and sometimes by a quarter berth or two tucked under the cockpit seats. Cabinets that serve as a galley area may be placed near the cabin steps or they may be forward to separate the bunks. For privacy there is sometimes a full bulkhead between the forward bunks and the main cabin. Offshoots of this layout may include an enclosed head compartment on larger trailerable sailboats, and perhaps a dinette to replace one of the settee berths.

For the majority of trailerables, you don't want more than four people. If it is one family with three children, you'll get by. But there is a limit to the number of people who can fit inside and still remain friends. As one man told his builder after having owned big boats, "Make it drink six, eat four, and sleep two." That way he could be hospitable *and* comfortable.

Taking an already small space and chopping it up into smaller segments is a curse that the designer has to face, especially when buyers ask for a bulkhead for privacy. In some instances, the privacy can be achieved by a curtain which can be pulled back to open up the cabin, but that isn't always satisfactory. Many people simply prefer the slightly smaller feeling of a cabin with a bulkhead than the open and public feeling on boats without the wall.

You'll probably form your own impressions during that first moment inside the cabin, but here are some points to consider while looking around.

First, is there enough headroom? There are two schools of thought on this subject. One says that headroom is useless unless you're planning on dancing or you need to stand while pulling on your pants. The other says that headroom is absolutely necessary even in a small boat. Decide what you want and see if it's enough for you. Bear in mind that most of your time below will be spent either sitting or lying down. The cooking functions can be handled by sitting next to the galley on a low boat.

One method that designers employ to have their cake and eat it standing up is the so-called "pop top." This is a section of deck that hinges upward over the main cabin area when the boat is at rest. In most cases, a fabric windscreen attaches so that the end result is an enclosed area with full headroom. The drawback to this is that you still have the low cabin when you're under sail, and you have more places for leaks to occur when you enlarge and complicate the hatch. But most people with the pop-top option think it's a great solution.

Take a look around the galley area. It won't be like home, unless you live in a closet, but it should have the basics. Probably the most important thing to check is counter space. Is there enough to lay out a spread of peanut-butter sandwiches without doing them all one at a time?

Some trailerable sailboats have a built-in space for the stove, while other simply place the stove on top of the counter and thus reduce the useful working area. If the stove is built in, see if it is gimbaled to swing level while under sail. That makes brewing a pot of coffee or heating soup much easier on a cold afternoon, although you can add a separate gimbaled stove for just that use.

The icebox will be examined more thoroughly later, but check now to see if it seems reasonably sized. Don't forget that you won't be putting just food into it, but you'll need enough space for a block of ice as well. Will it hold enough for your family on a weekend, and is it comfortable to use? Some iceboxes are simply deep pits, and the item you want is always on the bottom. The best iceboxes open from the top (to release a minimum of cold air), have a built-in space for the ice, and are shelved for easy access.

The sink, if built-in, should be deep and narrow for use when the boat is heeled. The standard shallow bowl that would be fine in your boudoir just slops water on everything in a boat. If the sink doesn't seem big enough, you can always replace it later with a deeper version.

This artist's rendering of the Venture 222 shows the pop-top cabin in the raised position, but without the protective canopy used in bad weather or for privacy.

This boat has a "hideaway galley" arrangement that stores out of sight when not in use. The stove is on the port side and the sink, with a self-contained water supply, pulls out from the starboard side.

Since the main reason for having a cabin is to provide a place to sleep, don't hesitate to try out the bunks. For the average person, a bunk of less than 6 feet 3 inches is too short, even if you're only 5 feet 10 inches. That still only gives you five inches for your pillow, and, believe it or not, people are taller when lying down because their feet relax and point downward. The width of the bunk is just as important as the length, and 30 inches is the recommended minimum. Anything less and you'll feel like you're going to fall off the bunk, especially if you have broad shoulders. But length and width aren't all there is to a good bunk, and you should check for vertical clearance. There are a few boats around that don't have enough space over the bunk to permit sleeping on your side.

This compact trailerable has the galley cabinets mounted between the forward and aft bunks. The stove stores in the cabinet under the sink, and the starboard cabinet holds an icebox.

Take a look at how the bunks are laid out and see if it fits your needs. If you plan to cruise with three kids, two of them probably won't want to share a double berth made from the dinette. You'll be better off in that situation with three singles.

The V-berth arrangement forward absolutely defies sheets and blankets, but check it for length as well. You'll want a filler piece to place between the open ends to form a full berth for extra space. If the V berth isn't longer than a normal bunk, you'll have tangled feet all night.

Many trailerables incorporate a dinette into the layout, although this has both pros and cons. Those who like the dinette say that it's useful for cooking (as extra counter space) and it makes a good place to eat when below. These are usually couples, however, who never need to seat more than two people at a time. Those who dislike the dinette say that it takes up more space than it is worth, that they rarely use it and prefer to eat in the cockpit, and that it doesn't seat enough people to justify its being there. If the dinette is an option, see if it fits your plans before you order it. If it comes standard, see how easily it converts into a bunk.

Check the light and air inside the boat. These are both critical for a comfortable interior. There should be plenty of portholes or windows in every compartment to allow the maximum amount of natural light inside. Besides making the cabin bright and cheerful, the ability to look

This larger trailerable has more space and separates the forward and aft cabins with a bulkhead. In place of the settee bunk to starboard, a dinette has been fitted. When the stove is not in use, the white panel behind it folds down to create additional counter space.

outside is a prime way to reduce seasickness. Make sure the builder hasn't stinted on portholes. If you put four people in a closed cabin, you'd be surprised at how quickly the air can become ripe. At worst, there should be a full opening forward hatch that hinges upward and a main hatch that can be left open. The next step in ventilation is to have opening portholes that allow air to flow through. And the last step is to include ventilators on deck, but these are usually options.

You'll want to give the head, or toilet, a once-over, because it will be important to your future cruising. In many modern trailerables, the head is removable for emptying ashore. This isn't simply for convenience, but because there is such a maze of regulations covering holding tanks, methods of emptying, and so forth that it is easier for everyone to install a simple chemical toilet like those found in motorhomes.

The ultimate luxury, of course, is an enclosed head compartment, but most trailerable sailboats simply have the head installed under one of the forward bunks. The drawback is that the head can't be used when anyone is sleeping in the berth, while an enclosed or separate head permits use at any time.

Construction

Although there are a few wooden trailerable sailboats around, for the purposes of this section we'll be dealing strictly with fiberglass, which accounts for 99 percent of the boats in this category.

Hailed as a miracle material, fiberglass is often overrated and generally misunderstood. An elementary knowledge of fiberglass construction is helpful to the new boat buyer, since a fiberglass hull is much more difficult to judge for quality than wood.

Fiberglass laminates basically consist of two components: the reinforcing material and the resin which permeates the material and hardens. The reinforcing takes several forms: fabric (clothlike weave); mat (random fibers); and roving (coarse weave). Application methods also differ: some builders produce the hull by hand "lay-up" with layers of roving, mat, and cloth, while others spray on a mixture of random fibers and resin from a "chopper gun," similar to the Gunite spraying of a swimming pool.

The fiberglass deck of a trailerable sailboat being lifted out of the mold. From this point, it will have some fittings bolted onto it, and then it will be attached to the hull for finishing.

As you make the rounds of boat dealers, you'll hear a lot of wild assertions about the properties of chopper and hand lay-up. But Owens-Corning Fiberglas notes that their labs have data showing that some chopper gun methods (which are usually claimed to be weak) are actually superior to hand lay-up, but they emphasize the importance of the workman. As one expert noted, "The builder is alloying the material, and the buyer should look at it in those terms. It's not so much the material or the method, but the guy who does it."

Fiberglass is several times as strong as wood planking, yet about the same weight as aluminum. Fiberglass eliminates caulking between planks as well as the need for wood preservatives, although the idea that fiberglass never needs painting is a myth. Fiberglass color is created by gel coats on the outer surfaces, which will dull and craze with time, necessitating a cosmetic paint job.

The fiberglass liner of a trailerable sailboat before being bonded into the hull of the boat. All bunks, cabinets, and storage areas are molded into the liner.

Three main problem areas are inherent in a fiberglass boat: stress concentrations, joints, and attachment points. Stress concentrations are areas where something will join a glass hull or deck, such as a bulkhead. Since fiberglass is flexible, the hull will bend while the rigid bulkhead will remain solid, which causes a fatigue weakness. Quality construction spreads the loads from a stress concentration over a large area.

The biggest problem of most fiberglass boats is the hull-to-deck joint. A quality builder usually attaches the deck with bolts (not pop rivets) and then goes back and bonds it with fiberglass for strength and waterproofing. Attachment points where a piece of hardware joins the hull or deck, such as cleats, engine mounts, masts, and shrouds, should be engineered to take that particular load, plus a reasonable safety factor.

When looking at a new fiberglass boat, the buyer will have trouble determining its quality. Finding an unpainted hull area and looking for edges that might indicate thickness or joints that show the bonding technique can serve as starting points. One surveyor suggested that the buyer look for other signs: "I give high grades to any builder who makes a tidy boat throughout. If you find a lot of sharp-edged fiberglass hanging down inside, then I wonder how the rest of the boat was built. This doesn't automatically condemn it, but certainly the builder ought to get credit for doing a neat job."

A fiberglass boat responds well to "tire kicking." A good laminate, when tapped sharply with a hard object like a coin, will make a crisp clear sound while a dull or muffled sound indicates the presence of uncured resins or air pockets.

Visually, a good fiberglass laminate is evenly translucent when viewed from inside toward a light source. Dry areas that lack resin content appear whitish, while air bubbles show up as dark spots. The surface gel coat is readily visible and is not a structural item, so small hairline cracks or bubbles that have popped are purely cosmetic and of little concern.

Foam and balsa cores, which add stiffness to long expanses of unsupported fiberglass, have their own problems. Balsa, being organic, is vulnerable to rot and water absorption, while foam is generally weaker and more unstable to work with than balsa.

Fiberglass also has some inherent problems that buyers have to learn to accept. First is an insulation problem since fiberglass readily transmits cold or heat. Second, it sweats like a beer bottle. Many boats have interior liners to protect the unwary yachtsman from a sudden droplet of cold condensation in the face late at night. The smell of fiberglass is often a gripe, although it does seem to go away with time. The noise level in a fiberglass boat is much higher than in a similar wood boat, primarily because of the thickness of the wood and the sound-transmission properties of the hard fiberglass. Fiberglass also burns very hotly, and a small fire can spread quickly through an entire hull.

The best place to start your construction survey is with the boat on the trailer. Take a look down the hull side and see how smooth it is. It doesn't require much expertise after you've seen a few boats to tell the difference between a ripply fiberglass hull and a smooth one. Despite some claims made by manufacturers, a hull with ripples or waves isn't necessarily weaker than a smooth one, but it does indicate that the builder did a quickie job when making the original mold. The hull may

The deck mold of a trailerable sailboat with a deck in the process of construction. The fiberglass is complete, and the workmen are adding the plywood stiffening and back-up plates under the deck.

be strong, but the manufacturer may also have scrimped in other areas besides the mold.

What you can look for as you sight down the hull are hard ridges where a bulkhead joins the hull on the inside. This indicates that the builder merely glassed the narrow edge of the bulkhead to the hull, causing a stress concentration and a potential crack. Joints should have overlaps of about 6 inches to distribute the stress.

Climb up on the boat and stroll around the deck. Check it for stiffness or firmness. A soft or spongy deck is an indication of either shoddy craftsmanship or inept design. There is no excuse for a deck that flexes under your weight. Take a look under the deck and see if the stiffening material is plywood (which is prone to rot), balsa, or foam.

Looking around inside the cockpit, you can probably poke your head into a cockpit hatch and look for the thicknesses and translucency tests mentioned before. Check for rough or sharp edges, and make a visual judgment of the general quality, especially in areas that aren't readily visible.

While you're in the cockpit, now is the time to survey it. Take a look at the seats and flooring, and make sure that the nonskid pattern is good. There is a fine line between a good nonskid and a bad nonskid. Bad nonskid is usually of such a shallow pattern that it doesn't give your shoes a good grip and a layer of water makes it slippery. It can also be the opposite, with a pattern so coarse that it is uncomfortable on bare feet and wears out the seats of your clothes. Good nonskid has a well-defined pattern, but is not sharp to the touch.

Look at the cockpit seats, and make sure that they slope so that they drain easily. Besides being easier to clean, a well-drained seat prevents you from sitting in a puddle. Look also at the drains in the cockpit floor and make sure that they are sufficiently large to empty out any water that fills the cockpit. Ideally, the drains should have about a 2-inch inside diameter to empty a lot of water, but you'll probably be given 1-inch drains. Some cockpits drain directly through the stern, and these should have flaps to prevent water from washing back into the cockpit from the sea.

Lift the cockpit hatches (and any others molded into the deck) and make sure that there is a large lip to drain off water.

Lean back while you're sitting in the cockpit, and see if the wood or fiberglass coaming around the side is enough to support your back

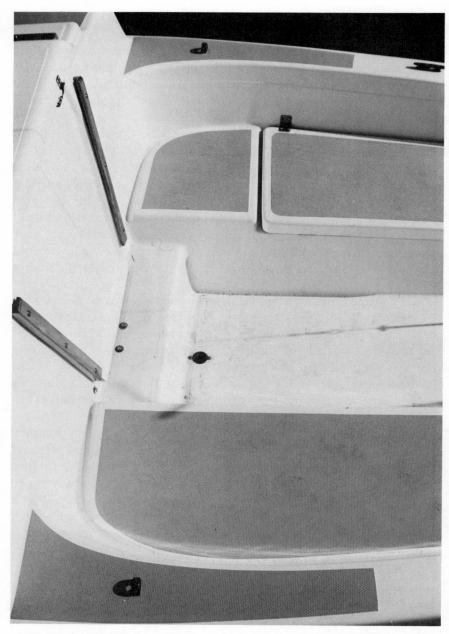

This trailerable has only a single cockpit drain, placed in the center of the cockpit where it won't completely empty the boat when heeled, but it does have good drainage from the back of the seats and around the hatch lips.

This view of the cockpit on a trailerable sailboat shows the cockpit drain, which is insufficient in size. It also is in the center of the cockpit so that, if the boat is heeled, there will be a large pool of water that cannot reach the drain. A better solution would be two drains of larger diameter in each corner of the cockpit to empty all water out quickly.

comfortably. You'll be spending a lot of time leaning back in this cockpit. Now is the time to see if it is too low.

While you've got your head stuck into the cockpit hatches, look up under the rail and see how the deck hardware is fastened down. The cleats and winches should be bolted through a backup plate to spread the load and then have either aircraft nuts or lock washers on each bolt. The next step down in quality is simply regular nuts and washers, but you should check them to see if they've vibrated loose. The lowest quality installation, and one that is unacceptable, is where the builder has omitted the backup plate under the hardware. This doesn't allow the load to be spread over a large area, and you shouldn't trust that piece of hardware or that builder.

On deck, look closely under the hardware to see how much sealant was used to bed and waterproof each item. There should be indications that the sealant wasn't used sparingly, since any microscopic openings will lead to annoying leaks later.

Check also the quality of the hardware, and find out if the material is stainless steel, aluminum, chromed bronze, or chromed pot metal. All except pot metal have a use aboard boats and should be from a major manufacturer so you can replace or repair the item easily.

Take a walk around the deck and inspect the life lines. Give the stanchions a hearty tug, and listen for the sound. You'll probably find that the stanchion will move, and this is normal. But a crunching or

This boat has good deep drain moldings to keep the cockpit floor dry, but the drains are so small that they would be hard pressed to keep up with a good rainstorm. Big drains would make this an excellent cockpit.

tearing sound indicates that there is no backup plate or that the fiber-glass is weak. The sound you heard was fiberglass tearing or crushing, and it means that the stanchion might not hold when you need it most. You're not worried about whether it will flex a little, but whether it will hold if an adult falls against it.

While you're next to the cabin, inspect the windows. Here, again,

This photo shows the best type of cabin window: firmly mounted in an alumi-num frame and well sealed to prevent leaks. It also shows the jib fairlead on the deck, which is an unsatisfactory way to lead the jib sheet. Because it can't be moved, you probably won't be able to get the jib to fill properly. The best method is to have a sliding fairlead (preferably a roller block) on a track to allow for adjustment.

there are several levels of quality. The best window installation is a shatterproof glass or plexiglass window mounted in an anodized aluminum frame. Often these are complete units that permit part of the window to slide open, and they are well sealed against leaks. A sign of low-quality construction is when the plastic window is simply bolted to the cabin side with sealant around the edge, a method that looks as poor as it works.

Stepping below into the cabin, you have several more areas to check for quality. Make a note of the general accessibility of various areas in case you need to make repairs. Some builders install all the deck hardware and then put the inside liner around the cabin to hide the bolts. It looks nice, but you can never remove or tighten the hardware.

Take a look into the bilge as well when you're checking for accessibility: there may be areas that the builder has effectively sealed off, which makes it inconvenient for the installation of depth sounders or for emergency repairs.

Look at the through-hull fittings. There are two lines of thought here for trailerable sailboats. One says that you must have seacocks or, second best, gate valves to shut off every underwater opening. In theory, this is fine because you may need to close off the opening when the pipe above it breaks. But the cost of bronze seacocks, as much as $100 each in smaller sizes, can mount alarmingly fast. The second line of thinking is that you should have gate valves only on openings leading to parts you may need to remove for repairs. This would mean your marine toilet, if it has an inlet or outlet, and it would allow you to remove the toilet while the boat is in the water. The recommendation for all other underwater openings is to have tapered plugs of soft wood that can be pounded into the opening in case of an emergency.

In either case, the tubing that leads to the through-hull fittings should have double pipe clamps facing in opposite directions for maximum safety. Don't be surprised if you have to add the second clamp yourself.

Take a general look at the quality of the interior woodwork, and you'll have a good indication of how much care went into the building of this boat. If the corner joints fit tightly and are mitered, then someone cares. If wood edges are splintered and don't fit squarely, then you know how important details are to this builder.

At the same time, check the drawers and cabinets to see if they open

At a modern boat builder, all the woodwork is preassembled and finished. When the fiberglass hull is finished, the woodwork simply drops into place.

readily and are finished properly. Look inside the cabinets and lockers to see if they have fiberglass or wood liners to protect your gear from contact with the bare and wet hull.

Give the electrical system the once over. All the different circuits should have fuses or, better yet, circuit breakers. There should be a master panel with a vapor-proof on-off battery switch, plus separate switches for the various circuits like interior lights, running navigation lights, spreader lights, and so forth. The battery itself should be firmly bolted in place inside an acid-proof container.

Make sure that the wires are also accessible and aren't buried behind a liner or, worst of all, molded into the fiberglass itself. Good-quality boats have the wiring neatly color-coded and then securely led throughout the boat in harnesses, where it can be checked and replaced. This is a good time to see if there is ample interior lighting. You won't be happy trying to read in your bunk if there is only one light in the cabin. Besides lights over each bunk and in the head compartment, you'll need lights in the galley area.

Most trailerable sailboats have a built-in water tank, and you should inspect it for material and installation. Some types of fiberglass and plastic tanks will flavor your water, and you'll never be able to rid yourself of it. The best tanks have a large access port in the top so that you can scrub the tank out occasionally to keep it clean and fresh. And the piping to the sink pump should be of a taste-free polyvinylchloride or similar material.

As far as the quality of the sailing gear, take a look at the mast and rigging. Since each boat has individual loads and requirements, there is no set size for mast diameter and thickness. But, after looking at several boats of the same size and type, you'll be able to make a judgment about whether the mast is the proper size. It's one area that builders often cut corners on under the assumption that they can always blame the buyer for bad seamanship if the mast breaks. If you question the size, check with owners to see if they've had any problems.

The rigging wire can be terminated in one of two ways: by Nicopress or by aircraft swages. Nicopress fittings are metal sleeves that are crimped onto the wire using an oversized pliarlike tool. They are good for the strength of the wire if properly applied, although they are not as neat as aircraft swages.

The aircraft swage is a machine compressed sleeve that has the correct end fitting built into it. It forms a rigid joint and, where the wire exits, it can produce fatigue breakage if care is not taken to keep the wire from bending.

Inspect the chain-plate installation carefully, since this is essentially

The mast assembly shop at a builder of trailerable sailboats. The aluminum extrusions are converted to spars here, and all the rigging is added at this point.

all that supports your mast. The chainplates should be bolted firmly to the hull and a structural member inside the hull. A fairly common shortcut that builders use is simply to bolt the chainplate to the hull alone, which often isn't strong enough to withstand the load and can actually tear open. Another poor-quality practice is to bolt the chainplate to the deck itself, which can pull loose from the hull.

If you plan to beach your boat often, you'll probably want a kickup rudder, which swings up in shallow water yet allows you to steer. It probably won't be as strong as a conventional rudder, though, so don't order it unless you need it.

With the normal swing keel on the trailerable sailboat, you'll want to look at the keel installation. There will be a winch so that you can

The shroud on this trailerable sailboat is secured with a pair of Nicopress swages to hold the wire. A metal thimble is also used inside the loop of wire to prevent kinking.

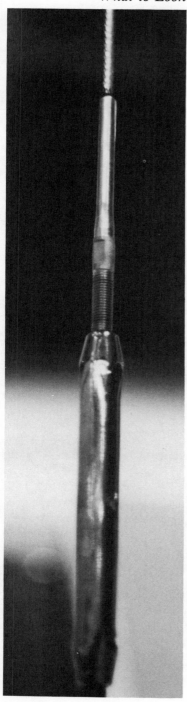

This shroud is secured with an aircraft-type swage with a threaded end that matches up with the barrel on the turnbuckle, a smoother but more expensive method than a Nicopress loop.

crank up the heavy keel for beaching or trailering, and you should make sure that it is geared for the task. Otherwise, your family won't be able to operate it without your strength. The cable itself should be protected from chafe since it will bear considerable load. Some manufacturers route the keel wire through a circuitous maze to keep it out of the way, which makes replacement difficult. A simple and well-protected keel and wire arrangement is what you need.

You should also check to see how the wire joins the keel itself. If it is imbedded into it, replacement may be difficult. Best is to have an eye bolted into the keel for the wire.

Make sure that there is a keel lock to hold the pivoting keel in its fully

Some trailerable sailboats are delivered with stay adjusters rather than screw-type turnbuckles. The adjusters are easier to use in stepping the mast, but they have less adjustment than turnbuckles. The headstay should always have a turnbuckle for the final tuning.

down position. A few unfortunate incidents happened to one type of trailerable sailboat that didn't have this provision. In a gust, the boat would heel far over and the keel would fold up, preventing the boat from righting. The addition of a locking pin could have avoided those accidents.

Regardless of whether you are a novice or an expert, you need a rub rail around the outside of your boat. The best rubrails are an aluminum frame with a tightly fitted rubber insert that won't pop loose or stretch. These will take a great deal of chafe and abrasion and still look good.

As a last check for quality, take a look at several other boats from the same manufacturer after they're a year or two old. That's the best way to foresee what problems you may encounter later. Look for cracked fiberglass, broken fittings, indications of repairs, or other signs stemming from the original construction. And don't hesitate to ask the owners—as long as they don't have their boat up for sale!

Storage Space

Storage is something that there is never enough of on any size boat, but particularly on trailerable sailboats. So it's something you need to review carefully before you make your decision on a boat.

Stowed inside your hull, preferably neatly, will be sails, anchor and line, your clothing, tools, food, engine and fuel tank, books, navigation equipment, sleeping bags and pillows, and any other items you choose to take along.

One useful trend on small boats is a built-in anchor well on the foredeck with a lifting hatch. The anchor and its rode can store in this well and not take up any interior space at all. An overboard drain allows the wet anchor gear to dry without filling the bilge. If the boat doesn't have an anchor well, it might have a storage bin forward of the V berths. But this isn't nearly as satisfactory.

Inside, take a look around the galley area and see how much usable space there is. Often there is only a token drawer and a token cabinet, neither of which is large enough to hold the utensils, plates, and cups that you'll want aboard. And don't forget that you'll have pots, pans, cleaning supplies, and all the little items that make a weekend a pleas-

The anchor locker on a trailerable sailboat is a handy way to keep a wet anchor
and line out of the way but ready for immediate use. The locker has a drain
that empties water overboard.

ure, ranging from corkscrews to salt shakers. Unless you're really ready
to rough it with a bag of paper plates, you'll need someplace to put your
galley gear.

Most trailerable sailboats won't pass this simple test. So, rather than
give up, you need to consider how to improve your future boat in this
department. We'll look at specific changes you can make later. For

now, give some thought to your needs.

When you're looking at drawers and cabinets, make sure they have positive latches. Otherwise you'll find everything on the floor when the sailboat heels in an afternoon breeze. Most drawers have a simple gravity notch so that you have to lift the drawer slightly before it will slide out. Cabinet doors are more complex. A simple magnetic or spring latch is not good enough to hold a load of pots and pans. One common method is to put a metal latch on the inside of the door and then drill a finger hole through the door for access. This is fine, as long as you don't lose your balance, which can cause a broken finger. The best latch system is a wooden toggle that swings down to hold the door shut and pivots up to open it. A sliding bolt is also acceptable.

Give bonus points to boats that have ample food storage areas, particularly if these areas are sealed off from the rest of the boat. Too often, the manufacturer simply fiberglasses a cabinet onto the inside of the hull, which allows condensation to form in the locker that you use for sugar, salt, and crackers. Guess what the result is? Look for fully lined cabinets away from either the hull side or the bilge area.

Once you've reviewed the galley area, move on to your personal needs. With a family of four, you'll need quite a bit of space, which probably won't be there. Again, most builders leave the details up to each owner to personalize the boat for his own needs. One area you can check is hanging lockers (closets to the novice), which have room to hang coats and other bulky clothing as well as your good outfit for going ashore without wrinkles.

Check to see the actual size of the hanging lockers, and take off your jacket to measure them. A few boats have hanging lockers that are neither wide enough nor long enough for any jacket used by anyone past the age of ten. The locker has to be deep enough to take the full shoulder width, and there should be enough height so that the bottom of the jacket doesn't hit the floor or hull and get wet.

Take a look around the cabin for built-in shelves and lockers. You'll usually find lockers under each bunk, but these are simply hatches cut to allow you access to the bilge. Anything you store under the bunks should be waterproof, rustproof, and rarely used. This is the place to store spare parts and even tools if they are in a waterproof case. Don't let the salesman tell you that you can keep your clothing under the

This hanging locker is deep enough and wide enough to hold a full complement of coats without getting them wet, but the shelf will be difficult to reach. The bin at the bottom of the locker is useful for bulky items as well as shoes.

bunks unless each locker is lined to keep it dry.

Shelves will get taken up quickly with the often-used items such as binoculars, charts, flashlights, and so forth.

Using the suggestions above, you've probably come away disappointed with your prospective new trailerable yacht. "It just doesn't have enough storage," you wail. You're right, but it isn't the end of the world. If you're at all handy with tools, you can build a lot of storage that the builder omitted to save money. And if you usually hurt yourself on home projects, there are several companies whose business is to supply you with prefinished drawers, shelves, cabinets, and lockers. All you have to do is screw them into place, and you have more storage.

Price

It would be nice to leave price out of the considerations for a new trailerable sailboat, but for the majority of people, it wouldn't be realistic. We all have budgets, and these limit the price of the boat that we can consider and buy.

But there are some good things about prices, too. For one thing, you can control it by being well prepared and careful about how you buy your new boat.

At this point, with the cost of petroleum and petrochemical products such as fiberglass spiraling steadily upward, you can make your boat purchase a protected investment with a good expectation of recovering what you put into it.

If you buy wisely, according to observers dealing with marine finance, you can expect to get back the full purchase price in two to three years, assuming that you have kept the boat in good condition. Unfortunately, this doesn't apply to any boat at any time and at any place. There are a few ground rules that you need to keep in mind when you start planning your boat purchase as an investment rather than as a frill.

(1) Buy from a respected manufacturer. What you are looking for is a builder who has developed, over a reasonable period of time, the reputation for quality construction and good design. As this book is being finished, several major sailboat manufacturers have closed their

doors, so even the biggest builders aren't immune to financial disaster. You can look at their reputation, though, and you'll still be protected if the boat they built was good.

(2) Watch for introductory model pricing. It's an amazing fact that the majority of boatbuilders don't know exactly what each boat costs until they've built a few of them. They know how much it *ought* to cost, but the early list prices are often below even their own costs to produce the boats. In other cases, builders will offer the first few boats as loss leaders to stimulate interest in a new design, relying on the fact that later buyers, once interested, will pay a bit more when they've made up their minds.

But if you've done your homework and are ready, you can make an instant profit just by buying one of the first boats. If, for example, the first boats list at $12,000 and then the price jumps in three months to $15,000, you've made an instant $3,000.

There are some dangers to buying the first boats, however. The builder often uses the first boats to sort out his production line, and you may not get the quality that later buyers will receive. You also may have problems that are cured on later boats. There is also a slight risk that the boat may not prove popular, but, with a reputable builder, you don't stand much danger from those possibilities.

(3) Watch for closeouts. At the other end of the scale, large discounts are often available on boats that are being discontinued. Manufacturers sometimes allow dealers to mark down the last boats they have in preparation for the arrival of a new design as a replacement. The only danger here is that you should watch for a boat that may not have been popular and thus is being discontinued. But the builder is often just "updating" his model line to reflect new trends, or the new line may be only a minor change from the old line. In those cases, climb aboard the bandwagon and get the discounts. There are many buyers who have found that a five-year-old racing design, now outdated, makes a terrific cruising boat at a much reduced price.

(4) Buy from inventory. In the marine business, the manufacturer actually sells each boat to the dealer. Once delivered, it becomes the dealer's boat, and he has to pay for it. Usually he arranges "flooring," which is a bank loan made on a monthly basis at a high rate of interest. Therefore, the dealer is paying his own money, plus a lot of interest, simply to have that boat sitting on his showroom floor. If it's been there

for a few months, you can bet that he's ready to sell it so that he can get a newer boat that may move faster into the showroom. The drawback is that you're going to have to accept the color and the options, but you may also save enough to make it worthwhile.

(5) Keep an eye open for price changes. Sometimes there will be two boats on the same showroom floor at different prices: one delivered to the dealer before a price increase, the other one after the increase. Many dealers will simply boost boat prices to the new rate and keep the difference, but, if you know what the price used to be, you can hammer the dealer back down again. There is also the possibility that, if you order a boat rather than take one off the floor, a price change may increase the price you pay upon delivery.

(6) Shop around. Don't be embarrassed about telling the dealer that you're going to see what other dealers can offer you. He's in business to sell boats, and his prices are the same as other dealers. If they're willing to sell more boats by cutting the price a bit, then you should certainly buy from them.

(7) Keep an eye open for demonstrators. A boat that has been used for a few months as a demonstrator is often available at a large discount. You'll probably get a boat that is pretty well equipped (the dealer wants to show it off, right?) and that has been well maintained (same reason), but that may be a little used. The sails won't have the new crackle, the cushions have been sat upon, and you won't have your choice of color. Again, the price difference is often considerable.

(8) Check the used-boat market just the way you'd check the stock market reports, especially when you've narrowed your choice down to one or two boats. Make it a practice to read the classified sailboat ads in the newspaper, and get an idea of what similar (and identical) boats are worth on the used market. You may find that used boats are going for almost new prices, which means that a new boat is a good buy. Or you may find that used prices are far below new prices, which should alert you. Either the boat is a dog and owners are trying to unload, or you might consider looking at used boats and saving some money.

(9) Don't accept factory prices as gospel. Often the dealer is prohibited by his contract from discounting the boat itself. But he may be willing to throw in an outboard, a spinnaker, or a trailer, which, while it doesn't offend the builder, still cuts your costs.

As you fight through the offers and counteroffers, keep one thought in mind. According to the publisher of a nationwide guide to used-boat prices, every quality boat from a reputable manufacturer that was built within the last ten years has appreciated a minimum of 25 percent, which makes your new boat a sound investment!

The Builder

Mention has been made several times in this book to "reputable manufacturers." Like judging the sailing ability of a boat when you can't sail, finding a good builder is difficult. It takes instinct, the ability to ferret out gossip, and the perseverance to check facts. Even a Dun & Bradstreet rating won't tell you if a builder is good, because it rates only the financial stability and even that is shaky, judging by the D&B boatbuilders who have folded. But there are reasons for searching out a good builder.

First, a nationally known manufacturer helps protect your investment. The thousands of dollars he spends to sell the new boat will also help you sell your used boat when you're ready. Having the builder's name in front of the boating world certainly doesn't hurt your bargaining leverage when you resell.

The exception to this is the small, quality local builder who may be known in only a surrounding area. Often his reputation will spread without advertising, but you're probably best to resell his boats in their own territory rather than moving across country to an area that has never heard of him.

Second, the builder can help you find replacement parts and provide warranty service. Few parts are custom-made on trailerable sailboats, and you can probably find replacements even if your builder has folded; but it makes life easier if you can find everything at one place. Warranty work will probably be done by the dealer, but he may not be willing to do it if he can't get reimbursed from a defunct builder.

The dealer is almost as important as finding a good builder. After all, the dealer is your liaison with the builder for price, delivery, and the resolution of any problems. If the dealer can't or won't fulfill the warranty, you're stuck.

Thankfully, finding a good dealer is much easier than finding the boat itself. Word of mouth travels fast and, if you're talking to owners about their boats, you probably have already been given a few names to try and a few to beware of. Don't hesitate to ask about dealers. You'll get some interesting answers that could save you dollars (and grief).

Several dozen new trailerable sailboats are prepared for delivery at the McGregor plant in California, one of many builders producing thousands of trailerables every year.

4

~·~·~·~·~·~·

What to Order
with the New Boat

By now you've been inundated with brochures, magazines, newspapers, salesmen, and advice. Somehow, through this wilderness, you've managed to decide upon a particular boat and a particular dealer. If you think that's all there is to it, well, you have another surprise coming.

During all the showroom discussions and demo sails, there have been some casually guarded references to "optional equipment." Now that you're sitting across the desk with your checkbook ready, the dealer slides across a tidy list of several dozen options and asks you which ones you want. Even if you're buying a boat off the showroom floor and not custom-ordering it, you'll still get asked the option question because many of these options are dealer-installed.

What is an option? An option, just as in automobiles, allows the builder to assemble the boat on a production line and still deliver a custom boat to the buyer. Each buyer has different interests and needs, and the option list lets him tailor the trailerable sailboat to his own taste.

Some dealers order only the most basic options on the boat and then install the remainder themselves so that they get the full profit rather than sharing it with the manufacturer on each option. That isn't as bad as it seems, since the dealer has access to identical equipment in most case and he buys it at almost the same price as the builder.

But the question here is how best to use your money. Just checking off a few of the options on the list handed to you by the dealer can add as much as $5,000 to the cost of your new boat.

You need to decide which options you want and which options you don't need. Once you've weeded out the options you don't want, you can examine the ones that you've selected. Compare the price against your own ability to install or add the equipment. The savings can be considerable, and many smart buyers pare off all but the essential factory-installed equipment and then add the rest themselves. By doing that, they have eliminated all the labor costs, and they can often get discount prices on the equipment by buying it all at once from a marine hardware store or through a discount marine catalogue store.

The following list is a typical option list for trailerable sailboats. It's actually compiled from the price lists of more than fifty currently available boats, although each option list varies since some boats include as standard what other builders consider to be options. The list also has a price range to show the differences among builders and among the types of equipment.

Let's take a look at each option and see what is involved. Since options vary from builder to builder, be sure the dealer makes it clear exactly what is included with each option and then weigh it against your own ability and the equipment prices at a hardware store. In some cases, you may find immediate savings. A winch handle, for example, listed on an option list at $43 may cost only $40 in a marine hardware store. The $3 profit is to cover the builder's effort in putting it aboard for you!

OPTION LIST

Anodized/painted mast, $150–$350

Bilge pump, $75–$200

Bottom paint, $175–$250

Carpet, $75–$150

Chromed hardware, $75–$100

Cockpit cushions, $100–$125

Commissioning, $350–$500

Compass, $75–$200

Contrasting nonskid, $100–$250

Cowl vent, $40–$60

Curtains, $85–$100

Electrical system, $300–$450

Genoa gear, $100–$200

Halyard winch, $100–$125
Head, $150–$750
Icebox, $100–$150
Kickup rudder, $150–$200
Life lines, $250–$300
Mainsail cover, $50–$75
Motor mount, $95–$125
Opening ports, $40–$60
Outboard
Outhaul/Downhaul, $20–$30
Pulpit, $100–$175
Reefing gear, $35–$75

Sails
Shore power, $250–$350
Special hull color, $150–$300
Spinnaker gear, $200–$500
Stove, $90–$125
Vang, $35–$50
V-berth insert, $35–$75
Wheel steering, $700–$1,000
Whisker pole, $35–$50
Winch changes, $25–$100
Vinyl/fabric cushions, $100–$175

ANODIZED/PAINTED MAST. An anodized mast has been electrically coated to prevent the oxidation or corrosion of the mast. Anodizing does not need to be refinished like paint, although it can be scratched or abraded away with careless handling. It usually comes in colors such as gold or black. Painted masts have a coat of epoxy sprayed on the aluminum that is acid-etched for a good grip. The paint is available in many colors, although white and wood-tan are the most common. Paint will chip and scratch, but it can be touched up if damaged. If you plan to leave your boat in salt water or where the elements can corrode the mast, then you might consider either of these protections. But for the average trailer sailer, a coat of wax and a wipedown at the end of the weekend will provide good protection and a shiny mast for years.

BILGE PUMP. This is a necessity, but you should investigate what you get in the option package. Some builders mount the pump, route the inlet and outlet pipes, and install an overboard outlet. Others simply give you a pump in a cardboard box. A good bilge pump can easily be installed by anyone who can drill a hole, so you should check price here.

BOTTOM PAINT. This is an antifouling paint that is applied below your water line to keep marine growth such as barnacles from adhering to your boat when it's left afloat. Necessary only if you plan to spend extended periods on waters that encourage growth. Most prices seem reasonable, although you can add this at any time.

CARPET. This is usually a shag or indoor/outdoor carpet cut to fit the interior floor area of your boat. It's nice to have since it warms the interior as well as making the cold fiberglass floor suitable for bare feet.

This trailerable sailboat has two compasses mounted on the cabin for maximum visibility by the helmsman while racing or cruising. A speedometer is also mounted on the cabin.

Price is the consideration here. You can often do better at a local carpet shop in their remnant bin, since you don't have much area to cover. An afternoon with a razor blade can save you money.

CHROMED HARDWARE. Some builders install bronze hardware as standard and offer chrome plating as an option. This is strictly a dressy option, and those on a budget should stay away. After all, who's going to polish all the chrome?

COCKPIT CUSHIONS. Usually the price is best from the factory, unless the boat is highly popular and local upholsterers are getting in on the competition. This is a worthwhile option, since you'll spend a lot of time in the cockpit and fiberglass seats get cold and hard quickly. Get the thickest cushions available, so they can double as bunks in good weather.

COMMISSIONING. Though often listed as an option, you usually can't buy the boat without it. It's like "dealer prep" when you buy a new car. Depending on the dealer, it can be just an extra charge or you can get a legitimate commissioning where the dealer checks everything carefully. You should get, in writing, a list of all that the dealer will do for his dollars. This is an area in which you can probably haggle, especially if the dealer is only going to rinse off the boat.

COMPASS. Depending on where you plan to sail, this could be a necessity or an extra. Either way, it can be added when you decide you need it, and compasses vary considerably in price and style. The factory price is usually higher than you would pay at a hardware store.

CONTRASTING NONSKID. This is a dressy option, but it does have several points in its favor. You'll probably be ordering a light-colored deck such as off-white or white to keep the cabin cool and improve the looks of the boat. By having the nonskid areas tinted a slightly darker color, you still retain the effect, but dirt caught in the nonskid will not be as noticeable. It also improves the looks of most boats, and you'll probably recover the cost at resale.

COWL VENT. If this option is offered, it usually means that the factory has found that the ventilation inside needs help from this small deck vent. Installed prices on most option lists seem to equal the vent price alone, but check to see what vent you get and how much you're being charged for installation. You may not need this if you sail in a cool climate, and you can add it later.

CURTAINS. This is one area that most people think is overpriced, espe-

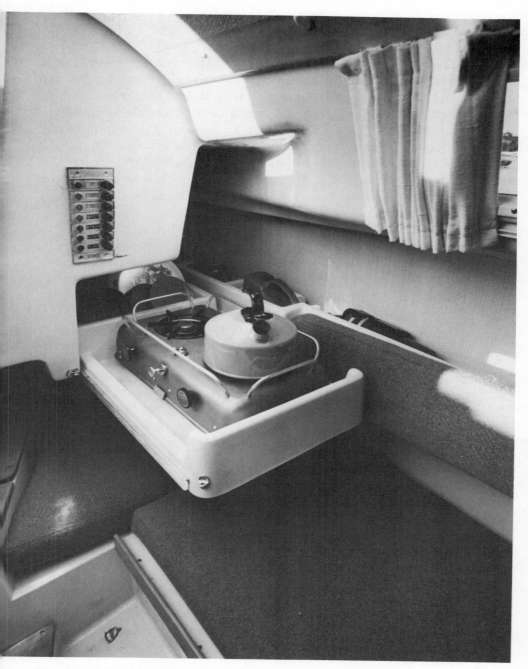

The electrical panel on the bulkhead is typical of most installations on trailerable sailboats. A master switch will be located near the battery, and all lights will be controlled from the fused panel.

cially if someone in your house can sew. The curtain rods are usually screwed or glued to the headliner above and below the windows, and the curtains are double-hemmed so they slide. You can probably do better, although the factory will match the interior colors and fabrics. ELECTRICAL SYSTEM. Unless you're a professional electrician, you're probably better off letting the builder install the electrics. The builder will put in the battery and master switch, a panel of toggles, and run the wiring throughout to lights and accessories. Make sure you know how many lights the builder will install, since dealers often add extra lights to their demonstrators for show purposes.

GENOA GEAR. If you plan to purchase a larger headsail either now or in the future, you might be wise to have this package installed. If you don't want the bigger sail immediately, see if they will install the genoa track alone, allowing you to purchase the rest of the gear later when you need it. That will cut your cost initially, but the job will be done right.

HALYARD WINCH. Unless you plan to race, you probably won't need a halyard winch to start with. It allows you to pull your jib up tighter and thus improve your windward performance. But there are less expensive ways of getting the sail tight, and you can add the winch later.

HEAD. Oh, boy. This is a real problem. The regulations covering what kind of marine toilet is legal are snarled and may remain that way for some time. Even if the rules are settled, the reality may stay just as complicated. Essentially, you cannot pump your toilet into any water in the United States, unless you have neutralized the sewage in one of several chemical or electrical ways. The other way to empty your head is to have it pumped out at a marine pump-out station, of which there aren't nearly enough. Portable toilets, used in many boats, can be emptied at home or elsewhere. You'd best buy the toilet with the boat, but ask your dealer what he recommends for your area. You may find that a few extra dollars spent to upgrade to a better toilet may vastly improve your disposition on a long cruise.

ICEBOX. Some builders offer this as an option and use the space for storage if you don't order the icebox. Take a look at the installed option, and see if it seems large enough and well insulated. If not, you'll probably do better to buy a camp-cooler-type ice chest and gain the extra storage.

KICKUP RUDDER. Good to have if you plan to sail in shallow areas or run up on beaches regularly. Worth the dollars if you plan to use it.

LIFE LINES. These are usually best installed by the factory since it has the right sized stanchions and the wires are plastic coated and cut to the correct lengths. Be sure to check the installation on other boats before you order, though, since you want hefty backup plates underneath and bolts through the deck itself.

MAINSAIL COVER. The prices for items that the builder subcontracts are always higher than on the outside market, and you can probably do better at your local sailmaker. You might investigate prices on do-it-yourself cover kits from various companies that provide precut material and you do the sewing.

MOTOR MOUNT. This is usually a bracket that fits on the stern, and the prices are only slightly higher than the actual hardware-store cost. You're better having the factory do it, since it knows the proper height and position.

OPENING PORTS. Like the cowl vent, this indicates you may need more ventilation. This is usually a low charge, since it is the difference in price between the standard windows and the opening windows. Sliding windows often leak, though, so keep that in mind if you're not sure you want opening ports.

OUTBOARD. This is definitely one area in which you should shop price. While your boat dealer is probably an outboard dealer, you may find a better discount price at a sporting-goods shop or fishing-equipment dealer who specializes in low-horsepower outboards. The warranty will be just as good regardless of where you buy it, so check prices.

OUTHAUL/DOWNHAUL. This is a block and tackle arrangement to give you some additional help in tightening the mainsail. The price is low enough that it's worth having installed by the dealer.

PULPIT. This is a worthwhile option, especially if you have small children or plan to do any cruising where you'll be anchoring for the night. Since pulpits vary, you'll have to check price versus quality. The best pulpits are all welded of stainless steel and designed just for your boat. Often the factory will provide this type. A pulpit of stainless tubing and chromed bronze joints that screw together doesn't look as good and usually wobbles. The installation can be done later, but not as easily.

REEFING GEAR. This is something that you should discuss with the sailmaker, since the sail has to match up with your equipment. Often, all the boats in one area use similar equipment, but check to be sure.

This is usually something that is inexpensive enough that you can have it installed by the dealer.

SAILS. Unless the sails are included in the basic boat, be sure to shop price. Often the dealer will aim you toward one particular sailmaker (usually the one who gives him the best discount), and you can sometimes beat that price by dealing directly. If you're buying more than a mainsail and jib to start, you can probably negotiate a package price or get an extra (like a mainsail cover) thrown in. Unless you're an avid racer, you might find that all sailmakers will do an equally good job for you. If you do plan to race, find a sailmaker who has had both experience and success in your class of boat.

The shore power connector on this trailerable has a permanent socket mounted outside the cockpit for the dock extension cord.

SHORE POWER. This allows you to plug in any equipment that requires household current (110 volts, A.C.). You'll get an outside plug in the cabin or cockpit side, a big yellow dock cord, and a couple of wall plugs inside your boat. At the price, you can run an extension cord. And, after all, how often will you be watching color television or using a mixer?

SPECIAL HULL COLOR. A dress option, again. The advantage is that you won't look like everyone else. But when you sell, you'll have to find a buyer who likes your choice. The price is less than repainting your boat, so order this if you can't live with standard colors.

SPINNAKER GEAR. A necessity if you plan to race, but just a frill if you don't plan to compete. Spinnakers are a lot of work to use, and your family may not appreciate the labor. All the gear can be added later if you want it, and you'll still have to buy the 'chute itself. The price usually varies depending on how complete the package is (some are only deck fittings, while others include everything but the sail).

STOVE. If the stove is built-in, you're probably better off ordering it from the factory. But if it simply sits on top of the counter, check prices and see if you can do better at the local marine store. You may even find a different stove that you like better.

VANG. Even if you're not a racer, this can improve your sailing and make your boat safer. It's not complicated, so see if you can do better at the marine hardware store. But you'd be wise to have it when you start sailing.

V-BERTH INSERT. On the typical trailerable, the aft end of the V berths (where your head and shoulders are) has an opening between the bunks. This filler makes the divider bunks into a large double, using the full width. It is a good idea to order from the builder, since the builder will match the fabric and mattress thickness. Useful if you want to use a single blanket up forward.

WHEEL STEERING. This costs a lot of money, and you don't really need the mechanical advantage that a wheel gives you. It responds slower than a tiller, but it does increase your cockpit space.

WHISKER POLE. Check the price against the discount stores. Usually the supplied whisker pole is a collapsible aluminum affair that requires only an eye on the mast. It's useful when you don't have a spinnaker, but you can make your own. One option is to find a dual-purpose whisker pole that has boat-hook fittings on one end.

WINCH CHANGES. Most builders offer buyers the opportunity to ex-

The V berths in the bow should have a filler cushion added so that they become a full-width berth to allow the use of a single blanket or sleeping bag as well as providing extra sleeping space.

change the standard winches for larger or fancier winches. You'll have to talk to the dealer and other owners to see if you really need to upgrade your winches. In most cases, the standard winches are suitable for cruising and limited racing, while the bigger winches are needed for serious racing. The price you pay is the difference between the standard and the larger winches, so order them now if you think you might want them.

VINYL/FABRIC CUSHIONS. Some builders offer vinyl cushions as standard, while others offer fabric ones, but most offer the opposite material as an option. Vinyl is easy to clean and cold to sleep on. It resists water and spray, and the cockpit cushions should be vinyl. Fabric cushions are warmer to sit and sleep on, but they don't like being wet and they won't wear as well as vinyl. The choice is yours and should be made at this point since it's an exchange price. One thing you should opt for if offered is thicker cushions. Anything less than a 4-inch mattress is too thin for the average person for sleeping, and some builders have 3-inch mattresses as standard with thicker cushions available. They're worth the price.

The most important thing to remember when going down the checklist is to compare the price against what you can get it for elsewhere. Just because the builder *can* install it doesn't mean he *has* to install it. Wise buyers find out exactly what is included, by brand name, and then take the option list to a local hardware store for price comparison.

You may be surprised to learn that some equipment is less from the builder (he gets a favorable discount) or considerably more. Be realistic about what you need and what you might want in the future. Have difficult items installed by the builder, and do the rest yourself. Then spend the money you saved on something frivolous.

5

~~~~~~~

What to Look For in a Used Boat

Because of the rapid escalation of new-boat prices, a great many buyers of trailerable sailboats seriously consider the used-boat market. But looking at a used boat is quite different from buying a brand-new boat right off a showroom floor, and even expert yachtsmen admit that it takes a sharp eye to get a good buy. Even more important, there are some specific things to look for in a used trailerable sailboat that don't apply when looking at more traditional yachts.

You've already made the basic decisions as covered earlier about the type of boat that you want and the amount you want to spend. Instead of finally deciding on one particular model, it's a good idea to keep several different boats as targets on the used-boat market so that you'll be ready when a good deal comes along. Just like buying a new boat, you'll also want to leave some of your boat budget in the bank so that you can add to your used boat or do some repair work on it.

Since you've already decided what kind of boat you want, be sure to stick with your decision. If you want a cruising boat, don't get excited about a trailerable loaded with racing gear that you'll never use. On the other hand, don't jump for a cruising boat because you'll have to add a lot of expensive equipment to go racing. When looking at used boats, always ask yourself: "What exactly am I getting that I don't need, and what do I have to add?"

Educate yourself just as you would if you were buying a new boat. Talk to dealers, owners, sailmakers, and repairmen. While talking to the new-boat dealer, find out what changes have been made in the boat since it started production. This can give you a good idea if there were possible problem areas that the factory corrected in later boats. At the same time, check to see if a new version is due out soon that might undermine the value of your used boat.

Prices of used boats can be misleading. If you've checked with the local dealer and found that a TS-25 sells for $15,950 new, then you might think that a used TS-25 in good condition for $15,000 isn't such a great buy. For $950 more, you can get a brand-new boat. But you have to consider equipment costs, which probably include trailer, sails, electronics, outboard, options, and other gear. That used TS-25 may turn out to be a real buy when you add another $5,000 to the new-boat price for the same equipment!

Marine surveyors are rarely called in to check over used trailerable sailboats, although a wise buyer will include a marine survey in his offer to buy. But initially, at least, you're going to have to be your own surveyor while you decide whether to make an offer or not.

As you first size up a used trailerable sailboat, start a list of what will need replacing, repairing, or adding. Make it as comprehensive as you can, so you'll have a good appraisal for impending costs beyond the outright purchase. Include the major items like an outboard overhaul or new sails, but don't forget to include the small things. Even little necessities, like replacing worn dock lines, can quickly add to your total investment.

Look the entire boat over. It doesn't take an old salt to tell if a boat has been cared for or not. Chips and gouges in the hull are hard to remove as well as expensive. Worn lines, rust stains, discolorations from puddles in the cockpit, and other indicators all point to a boat that needs work. It may be purely cosmetic, but it could also mean expensive repairs and replacements. Proceed carefully.

The best place to start your survey is on the trailer, just as when you looked at new boats. Check the hull sides for ripples or waves that indicate poor-quality molds. Watch for ridges where bulkheads join the hull, and examine the area closely for cracks or signs of fatigue.

At the same time, give the gel coat on the surface a look. Dull or chalky gel coat can usually be polished out with a rubbing compound, but it also indicates neglect. Keep your eyes open for large discolored areas that mark patches that don't quite match the original color. There is often no problem, but check inside the hull at that spot to see more of the repair quality.

You should wear old clothes for your inspection, because it's time to look under the boat. Does the trailer support the hull evenly, or is much of the weight concentrated on just a single roller or pad? If so, the boat may have developed a bend in the hull that can hurt performance and weaken the structure itself. Look also for scratches or gouges that might indicate careless operation. If there is no bottom paint, look for small etched marks left by barnacles. They don't affect strength, but they show that someone left the boat afloat for long periods without adequate care.

It's now time to climb up on the boat. Check the deck for stiffness as before, but this time a soft spot might indicate rot or delamination in the stiffening in the deck as well as poor construction to start with. Either way, there may be a structural problem that would be expensive to repair.

Give the cockpit area the same check that you gave new boats: cockpit drains, seat drains, and hatch drains. Peer up inside the lockers and see what the general condition of the unseen areas of the hull are.

The interior should get a good review, and pay particular attention to the electrical system. Ninety percent of all electrical problems can be traced to a piece of electrical equipment that was added to the boat by an unskilled owner. Look for wiring that isn't bundled neatly and secured. If the previous owner has added electrical accessories, check his workmanship. It might save you from a dead battery or a fire.

Look at the hardware and see if it is of the same quality as the original equipment. Any new items should be marine quality, and not chrome-plated pot metal, which soon develops blisters and peels. See how new hardware has been installed. It should have backing plates and be solidly bolted down.

More and more electronics are being sold to the trailerable-sailboat market each year, and you're bound to encounter some in your used-boat search. Don't be misled by old equipment, though. Marine-electronics shops will survey radios, depth sounders, and direction finders at a reasonable fee when you get serious, and most items are easily removed from the boat for such a check.

Inside the cabin, take a big sniff. The air should be just as fresh as it was outdoors. Any musty odors or other odd smells are usually a dead giveaway of mildew or rot, and even prolonged airing often can't rid a boat of them. Lift up the bunk cushions and look for dark brown spots of mildew on the cushion or the wood. Peer into lockers and cabinets for the same signs, and don't hesitate to lift up the carpet and look into the bilge. The bilge should be almost dry (where would water come from?) and be clean and fresh-smelling. Anything else is a sign of poor care and possibly of other problems such as rot in the wooden bulkheads or in the fabrics.

Check the head to see if it is an approved type that is currently legal. Many boats built within the last few years have toilets with expired approvals, and replacement can be expensive. You may also receive a fine for using a boat with an illegal toilet, so check this with care. If the boat has no toilet, make sure that one can be added easily. You'll want it.

Dig out all the sails and check them over carefully. It's fairly simple to tell if the stitching is in good condition and if the cloth is ripped or worn. The sails should be clean and reasonably white. If they're parchment colored, stiff with salt, and have dirty or rusty spots, then they probably haven't had good care and you may face a stiff sailmaker's bill. Don't just examine the sails on deck, though. You should hoist *every* one and look at it carefully. If you have any doubts, drop the sail off at a sailmaker you trust (not necessarily the one who made the sail) and get his opinion. It can save you a bundle later.

Look the rigging over at the same time as you check out the sails. Sight up the aft edge of the mast and see if it is straight. A bend might indicate it had been damaged by dropping. Look at the wire rigging and see if the swages are in good condition. If there are broken strands and cracked swages, you'll need to replace the rigging completely. Look at the blocks and see if they spin freely or if the bearings are worn out. Spin the winches, too, and see if they drag.

You've spent a lot of time poking and prodding this boat. Now it's time for a test sail. Don't ever take anyone's word for the actual performance of any boat, new or used. Launch the boat and wring it out. If possible, use it the way you plan to in the future—with three or four people aboard, in the same winds and waves, perhaps even at anchor somewhere. You'll soon find out if the cockpit is too cramped or the boat too unstable or the foredeck too slippery.

You've taken the boat out and you like it. It passed the scrutiny on the trailer, and it's within your price and need range. Should you plunk down your money? Not quite yet. You'd be wise to have a professional marine survey, and you ought to give your insurance agent a call. Find out if he'd like to insure this particular boat. He may be delighted with the business, but, on the other hand, he may tell you that they don't like to insure this particular boat because of losses they've had. Better to find out now than after you've bought it. If you're planning to finance the boat, check also with your banker for any problems he might foresee.

Last, before you hand over the cash, get an itemized listing of all the equipment that will transfer with the sale. The sale of more than one huge ocean-going yacht has fallen through when the previous owner decided to keep a barometer he'd grown fond of. With a trailerable sailboat, there are many things that may or may not be included: portable radio, utensils, spare parts, fishing gear, and so forth. Have the owner prepare a complete list. If it's not on his list, assume that he isn't selling it and adjust your offer accordingly. He can always add items to the list, but you can't get them once the deal is completed.

For most trailerable sailboats, the actual transaction is fairly straight-forward. Unless you're buying from a dealer, you'll be acting as your own broker. Study the following sections and get an idea of what takes place in a boat sale.

The Yacht Broker and How to Use Him

Should you buy from a private party or should you deal through a yacht broker? There's no ready answer, unfortunately. In many cases, large yacht brokerage firms prefer not to deal in small or trailerable sailboats. They would be spending just as much time on a trailerable as on a much larger sale, and they obviously would make more money on the big boat. But there are a number of brokers who do handle, and some who even specialize in, the trailerable sailboat.

The yacht broker is the marine equivalent of the real estate broker: he acts as a middleman between the buyer and the seller. In boats of the size discussed here, you'll probably be dealing with several brokers and simply going through the listing books until you find something interesting. On a large boat, a buyer will usually deal with only one broker who then checks around to find what boats are available. But for a trailerable, you'll probably have to do your own footwork.

Just as in real estate, the seller lists his boat with the broker and fills out a complete description of the boat and its inventory of equipment. The broker then advertises the boat and shows it to prospective customers—like you.

The primary argument against dealing through a yacht broker is that he charges a commission, usually 10 percent of the sale price. Just as in buying a home, some people feel that they can buy the boat for less if they deal directly. The fact is that sellers usually list their boats for the same price as a broker, and then keep the change themselves. Wouldn't you?

A second argument against brokers is that, with the exception of California, there is no licensing of yacht brokers at this time. California requires that boat brokers and yacht salesmen take rigorous tests on marine matters and the financial and legal aspects of title change. But elsewhere anyone can hang out a shingle as a broker. So you'll have to be wary of fly-by-night brokers. One way to check a broker's reputation is to find out if he belongs to a trade association. The Southern Yacht Broker's Association, for example, has entry requirements that almost amount to a license, and an SYBA decal means a reputable broker.

What exactly does the broker do for the 10 percent. First, he makes sure that the title to the boat is clear and that no liens are held against the boat. Consider the grief that you might have if you found out, after buying from a private party, that there are major debts attached to the boat—all passing directly to you.

The yacht broker handles the entire transfer of title, a process that can get extremely complex. The broker maintains a trust account into which he puts your deposit and all other money involved. During the sale, he prorates the taxes or other charges against the boat, such as insurance, dockage, etc. He deducts the cost of haulout or survey work, and pays for the new registration. At the end of the transaction, a set of ownership papers is delivered to the buyer and the seller gets a certified check, all neat and tidy.

How does a buyer work with a broker? Usually it starts with the buyer going to see the broker, who was chosen on the basis of reputation, location, and/or recommendation. The first thing that the buyer should do is be honest with the broker. Tell him your plans, the size boat you want, specific details he should know, and what your budget is. The more information you give him, the better he can help you to find the perfect boat.

He may have some boats on his own list for sale. Let him show them to you, and be honest in your comments about them. This will help him to further narrow the search. If you don't see a boat that interests you, he may call other brokers to check their listings.

Once you've found the boat that you like, you'll want to make an offer. Rarely does a used boat sell for the asking price. In most cases, the offer consists of either a lower dollar amount or the requirement that work be done at the seller's expense before the sale is completed. Either way, the out-of-pocket costs for the buyer will be less. A 10-percent deposit will usually be required along with the offer, which is written up on an Agreement to Purchase form, which you should read carefully.

Once you've made the offer, the broker will present it to the owner or the owner's broker. The answer can be yes, no, or perhaps. The perhaps simply means that further negotiation will be required, an increase in price or a decrease in the amount of work to be done. A good broker will represent you fully during these negotiations and work for a satisfactory and fair deal.

Once the offer is accepted, you can then request the sea trial. If all goes well, you should move on to the marine survey, which the broker will arrange. If both the trial and the survey prove acceptable, the deal will close and you are a boatowner. If they are unacceptable, then the negotiations will reopen to see if a lower price or more repairs might make the boat more attractive. For example, an offer is accepted by the seller, the sea trial is no problem, but the surveyor finds dry rot. Further negotiations might either lower the price or require the seller to repair the rot at his cost.

The Surveyor and What He Can Save You

"I don't need to know about surveyors until I buy a used boat" is the reaction many readers will have to this chapter. But these same people are the ones who will probably learn the hard way that they needed a survey on *any* boat purchase.

What is a marine survey? Going back to real-estate terms, it is a combination of termite inspection, plumbing and electrical report, and property appraisal.

A marine surveyor will poke, prod, and study your boat thoroughly, inside and out. Using a comprehensive checklist, he will go over the boat and inspect it for a variety of ills and present you with a written report.

The report will include an overall appraisal of the boat's market value (which you can compare with the asking price), and a list of findings and recommendations. This list will cover legal violations, equipment or structures that need replacement or repair, and a rough inventory of the boat's equipment.

Do you need a survey on a new boat? You bet. In many cases, that boat has just survived a major journey across country on a trailer. It may have been bounced or jolted enough so that problems have started to occur even before it hits the water. It may also have basic problems in construction or design that you may not otherwise find out about until too late.

But isn't that what the local dealer is for? Won't he check to make sure everything is in working order? Don't bet on it. First, he may not have the experience to check for structural problems from the delivery trip. Second, he's in business to sell boats. Would you expect him to confess that your new boat isn't well built or well designed?

So the smart new-boat buyer will always call for an independent opinion in the form of a marine survey. Before the final delivery passes to the new owner, the surveyor will thoroughly check out the boat. If it passes, then you can rest assured that your boat is ready to go. If he catches some problems, you can have them cured by the dealer before you make the last payment. Believe me, any dealer will be a lot more concerned about fixing your boat if he's still waiting for that last check!

Anyone who buys a used boat without a survey ought to have his head surveyed. In almost every case, the bank will require a current survey (within the last month or so) before it will finance a used boat. In addition, your insurance company will also require a survey before it issues coverage. So any idea of cutting costs by eliminating the survey is going to make your life more difficult after you've bought the boat, especially if it won't pass a survey and you've already paid the seller.

Last, the surveyor will provide a list of recommended repairs and replacements that is probably the best bargaining tool available. Any buyer that can't recover at least the cost of the survey by showing the seller all the problem areas in his boat just isn't trying very hard. Use the survey to bring the price down, and you'll also have the reassurance of striking a good deal.

How do you find a surveyor? Like brokers, anyone can hang out a shingle and claim to be a surveyor. Again, reputation travels fast on the waterfront, and you can talk to other recent boat buyers to see what their experiences have been with various surveyors. Your banker and insurance agent can supply you with a list of surveyors of whom they approve, and you should make sure that your surveyor is on their list. Brokers can also recommend surveyors, although you must be cautious because they want to sell the boat. Last, ask the surveyor about his background in trailerable sailboats before you hire him. Some surveyors specialize in freighters and tankers, and you don't want them trying to survey your little pocket sailboat.

How does a surveyor operate? First, he'll go over the entire boat carefully, checking the condition of the hull, rigging, sails, engine, electrical system, and perhaps even the trailer. Based on what he finds, he will then submit a report that lists his recommendations in categories of desirable and essential. For example, he may find no life jackets, and that recommendation is essential before the boat is legal. He may also find that the sails are worn, and a desirable recommendation would be for replacement within a year.

Once you have this written survey, you can go back to your Agreement to Purchase with the broker and decide if you still feel it is acceptable. Obviously, if the surveyor found major problems, you should cancel it immediately. But if there are small details that need fixing, you can simply revise the offer downward, or you can leave the offer as it stands with the proviso that the seller fix the problem areas before the sale.

What does a surveyor cost? In most areas, they work on either a per-foot or per-hour rate. From $4 to $8 per foot is the normal range, or $25 to $30 per hour. If travel is extensive, then there may be an additional charge for expenses. But for boats in the trailerable-sailboat–size range, a survey for $100 to $150 is a bargain compared to your potential losses.

In addition, you can help the surveyor do his work. Since you are paying the bill, you have a right to be present. Simply observing what the surveyor checks is an education and might be useful if this sale falls through and you have to start looking again. Don't slow the surveyor down, however, with foolish questions.

It's usually best if the owner is not present, because the surveyor will be more open about his comments. No husband wants an outsider to say that his wife needs cosmetic surgery, and no boatowner wants to hear his boat's problems. The best method is to have the owner present at the start to answer any of the surveyor's questions and so that he can fill in details about the history or use of the boat. But the seller should leave soon, so that the survey can be done speedily.

On a small boat, you can help by moving gear out of the way so the surveyor has full access. You can also lay out the sails, and put things back when he finishes. This will save him time and help familiarize you with the boat.

One last caution about surveyors. They aren't the absolute authority. The written report will probably have a clause that eliminates the surveyor's liability for any problems he misses. So don't expect to sue the surveyor if he proves to have been inept. Methods of survey differ, and many surveyors simply count the bags of sails rather than examine them carefully. They may judge the engine by external appearance and a short run, so they may miss some problems.

Use the surveyor as a tool, but don't expect him to be a prophet.

6

~·~·~·~·~·~·~

Commissioning Your Boat Properly

Commissioning is a salty term, and you've probably already found it included on the price list for your new boat. Traditionally, it means a thorough inspection of a large ship or naval vessel, a sea trial, and a formal delivery into service. The actual physical commissioning assures you that all contract specifications have been met and that the final product is of acceptable quality. Unfortunately, too many buyers assume a commissioning is only important with ships.

Along with the use of the surveyor on a new boat, one way that savvy boat buyers are getting their full value is to insist upon a traditional commissioning for their new boat. In many cases, although the charge for commissioning can be several hundred dollars, it's usually a quick "see, it floats" check when the boat is launched. This is followed by a hose-down to get the dirt off, and it has cost you a pretty penny.

But the lack of a formal commissioning and acceptance can lead to complex and expensive lawsuits, the nonpayment of valid warranty claims, and problems that remain unsolved.

Take the following case. Our buyer has chosen a Fineyot-23, and the dealer readies it at his dock. As the day ends, the work crew goes home and the buyer arrives for his first sail. Unaware that the rigging isn't finished, the dealer shows the buyer how to hoist the sails and waves a fond farewell after having relieved the buyer of his final payment. Minutes later, the buyer returns with a broken mast, a damaged hull from the falling mast, and some righteous anger. But the dealer contends that the delivery had taken place and he isn't responsible for the broken mast. Since the final payment has been made, he isn't too worried, leaving our buyer frustrated and angry.

Although most sales contracts refer vaguely to the commissioning, you should specify what is expected in writing and that the boat must be commissioned to your satisfaction. This becomes a promise of service, and is legally binding upon the dealer. The "satisfactory" clause allows you to have a variety of problems corrected, ranging from paint drippings on the deck to major repairs for damage occurring in shipment.

There are several facets to a good commissioning. Perhaps it is most effective to ask the dealer to notify you when the boat is ready for inspection. That gives him the chance to fully prepare it to the best of his ability. At that time, you can have your marine surveyor give it the once-over. If you request the survey too soon, the dealer will claim that he wasn't finished, but if he has said it is done, then you can be sure that it's ready.

Out of the water, you should have the boat thoroughly hosed down and you should check for leaks around the hull-to-deck joints, windows, hatches, and fittings. No water should enter the closed boat, and if it does, it should be repaired before you launch, even if it is a deck leak. There's no excuse for leaks. Check the bottom paint for full coverage, since the trailer pads may have unfinished areas beneath them. Last, make sure all the gear you ordered is aboard.

In the water, check the engine out completely and hoist all the sails to check fit and quality. Examine the rigging and the equipment with an appraising eye.

Finally, make a careful list of *all* cosmetic defects such as chips or bubbles in the fiberglass, cracks in the wood trim, and poor-quality chrome plating. If you ordered carpet, make sure it's clean. Too often the rigging crew uses it to clean their feet. And check to make sure that the interior of the hull has been carefully cleaned of all wood and fiberglass dust to save yourself that trouble.

Once you've finished the commissioning survey, type up the list of problems and present it to the dealer. Have him note on the list when the repair will be completed, and have him sign the list. By being businesslike but friendly, you will give him the impression that you expect him to complete the job in the same manner. On the same list, include all options or equipment that have not been delivered or installed and a due date for each.

Once you've gotten the signed list of all problems, sit back and let the dealer solve them. If he misses the due dates by a few days, don't worry. Delivery time and repair service in the marine industry are slow at best. But if you get continual excuses and broken promises, remind him that the written list and the dates are part of a contract that you expect him to fulfill. Wait a little longer, and then write the manufacturer and send a copy to the Better Business Bureau. This usually gets results, since the manufacturer will lean on the dealer.

As a last resort, you can have the repairs done independently and hire legal counsel to recover the costs from the dealer. If you properly prepared your original contract with the commissioning clause and the list of repairs, you'll win easily.

At a time when you're buying your first boat, you don't want to think about possible legal problems. But you'd be wise to cover yourself fully by using a surveyor and demanding a full commissioning. Most dealers work hard to give good service, but they will usually be less interested when you've made the final payment. Hold out until all the work is finished to your satisfaction, and you can be assured it will be done promptly.

Outfitting the Trailerable Sailboat

7

Sails and Covers

Next to the basic boat, sails will probably be the most expensive single item in your purchase. For that reason, and because they will provide your primary source of propulsion, you should take care to get a good set of sails.

Unfortunately, sails, like the engine of a car, are incomprehensible to the average owner. When it comes to deciding where the draft should go or why the engine is misfiring, he's lost. For that reason, it's best to call in a specialist for advice: the sailmaker.

When buying your new boat, the dealer will suggest two or three sailmakers as candidates for your order. These are often ones that give him the best discounts, so check around to see who is available and then pick a sailmaker.

Your best choice is a local sailmaker with a good reputation, particularly for sails of the size you're considering. In every case, it's not the dealer who takes care of your sail after the purchase, it's the sailmaker. The farther away the sailmaker is located, the more difficult it will be to arrange for him to look at a problem sail.

Talk to sailors in your area and find out which sailmaker has a good reputation. Every loft has a specialty of some kind: catamaran sails, cruising sails, dinghy sails, and so forth. Picking a sailmaker in the trailerable-sailboat field is wise in the long run, since that sailmaker is working daily with the inherent problems of your boat. A big-boat sail loft might overestimate the needs of a trailer sailer, and a dinghy loft might underestimate them.

Once you've decided on a sailmaker, use his recommendations (and those of the dealer) to decide on what sails you need. Examine your future plans carefully before you decide. Do you want to race, cruise, or both? Are you an experienced sailor or a first-timer?

For example, if you plan to cruise, then you can look for general-purpose sails and you might use a more durable fabric than the racing sailor. The cruiser will probably stick with the basic main/jib set, sometimes expanding to a genoa. If you have no plans for racing, then you should stay away from specialty sails such as drifters because they'll spend most of their time in the bag.

Remember that sails can always be added later after you've learned more about your new boat. Don't rush into any purchases. If you plan to race, for example, you might be wrong to order a general-purpose sail such as a medium genoa. After racing a bit, you might find that it's too big or too small, and you'll have to buy two sails to replace the one bad choice.

Experience is another factor. A beginning sailor should start with a simple sail and learn to use it, while a more proficient skipper can order goodies such as a zipper foot or fancy adjustments. In jibs, the rope luff is fine for the advanced sailor, but a wire luff provides a safety factor for the overzealous beginner who hoists the sail until something pops.

For the trailerable sailboat, a basic set of sails is the mainsail and the working jib. Mainsails are essentially alike, although there can be differences in methods of reefing for heavy weather and methods of changing the shape and draft. The working jib is small enough to be easily handled in most breezes, yet big enough to move the boat in light winds. It's basically an all-purpose sail, and many owners never add another sail.

The next step in your sail wardrobe should probably be a genoa jib, which is larger than the working jib and overlaps the mast by several feet. This gives you considerably more power in light airs as well as better speed when reaching. On the negative side, you might need larger winches to handle the load, and it may be larger than a family crew can easily handle.

From the genoa, the next step up, to the spinnaker, is a complex one. Made of lightweight nylon, the spinnaker is often used in racing (although some classes don't allow it) and it will increase your downwind speed. From a useful standpoint, however, it's more work than many families want for cruising, since it requires fairly constant attention plus considerable effort to raise and take down. Like the genoa, you'll need extra gear such as a spinnaker pole and all the lines to control the spinnaker.

There are also some other sails that may appeal to you, including drifters, reachers, staysails, and more. Unless you're a hot-blooded racer with considerable experience in this particular boat, wait before you order. Every boat responds differently to sail combinations, and you may order a useless sail based on your experience in another boat.

After you've made the basic decision on what sails to order, make sure that your dealer does more than just carry the sail bags aboard your new boat. Insist that he show you how to hoist and trim all the sails in a variety of conditions. One angry customer returned a mainsail to the sailmaker with all the reefing grommets torn out. Not believing that his sail was at fault, the sailmaker found that the dealer had not shown the customer how to reef the sail, causing the tears.

In recent years, package deals have become popular in the trailerable-sailboat field. A boat is offered complete with a set of sails, but, unfortunately, production-line sails have both good and bad points. A production-line sail is created when a manufacturer contracts to buy several hundred sails from a sailmaker in a mass order. The consensus of most sailmakers is that these sails are often inferior in shape and sometimes in quality to sails produced individually. Production-line sails are compromises—they have to be used in all areas, in all weather, and by every caliber of sailor. A production-line sail may end up in the gusts of San Francisco or the calms of Long Island Sound. Again, like cars, cost and quality are always joined together. But as long as you are aware that there are differences between production-line and custom-made sails, you'll be satisfied with your ultimate choice. A sailmaker simply can't afford to put his insignia on a sail that is bad.

If you're buying a used boat, take the surveyor's comments with a grain of salt. Rarely does a surveyor go to the trouble of hoisting each sail and checking the draft and general condition. Usually, he merely checks the bags of sails and estimates their condition and value. A more careful buyer should trace the background of the boat itself. For example, a boat sailed often in heavy winds will probably have worse sails than a sister ship used in light airs. Intensity of use is the key factor in sails. At the same time, a trailerable sailboat brought from another area for selling may have sails that are unsuitable in the new locale.

Look at the used sail when hoisted and eyeball it for worn spots where it hits life lines, spreaders, or stays. Check for worn jib snaps or sail slides, deterioration of grommets and luff wires, and torn bolt ropes. Look for tight leeches and worn seams. The stitching in a dacron sail is usually abraded first, since the threads don't sink into the cloth for protection as they do on cotton sails. The color of a sail is often a clue to its condition: a yellowed sail has seen a lot of sun and probably has tired cloth, since ultraviolet rays can shorten a sail's life considerably.

Although canvas and cotton are outdated for sailmaking purposes, the need for these and other heavy fabrics in boating is growing. Boat covers, awnings, sail covers, and so forth force the boatowner to understand the basics of canvas and similar materials.

There are three basic types of material used for boat covers and accessories: canvas, acrilan, and vinyl-coated laminates. Canvas is the least expensive of the three as well as being a dependable and traditional cover material. Marine grades of canvas are treated for mildew-prevention at the mills, are preshrunk, and are available in several weights and colors. A drawback to canvas is that, despite preshrinking, it will still continue to shrink slightly after fitting. A second disadvantage is that the average age of canvas in boating use is about four years. But because of its strength, canvas is an excellent material for use on trailerable sailboats, particularly if the boat is towed at highway speeds with the cover in place.

The second material is Acrilan, a synthetic weave that has much the same appearance as canvas. Acrilan is available in a variety of colors, although the most popular are a vibrant blue or an off-white. Acrilan has almost no shrinkage, is lighter and more easily folded than canvas, and has a life expectancy of about five to six years. Its most common form is only water-resistant, although it can be treated with a waterproof coating. Acrilan will not mildew, and about 80 percent of all new covers are made of Acrilan.

The last type of specialized cloth is a vinyl-coated laminate, usually a vinyl layer over either a nylon or dacron mesh base. This material is fairly expensive, completely waterproof, and is most often used for flexible spray dodgers or awnings. Because of its inherent stiffness, it is best used for items that don't need to be folded up or moved.

This photo shows a sail that shouldn't be trusted. It has been exposed to sun and weather for so long that the fibers are brittle and a new sail will be needed.

Before making any decisions on a cover, discuss your needs with a cover maker. Too often, a new boatowner will try to duplicate a cover that he had seen on a larger boat—with disastrous results. Just because a 40-footer has a canvas cockpit "room" with six-foot headroom doesn't mean that your 25-footer can have one. A reputable canvas maker will try to produce an item that is not only well made, but which fits the lines and needs of that particular boat.

When considering a boat cover of any type, give some thought to color and ventilation. A dark cover isn't much of a problem in a cold climate, but in a hot area it will absorb heat and bake the boat inside. Some sailmakers have advanced the suspicion that dark sailcovers are overheating the tightly rolled sails inside and cutting their life expectancy by large margins.

Ample ventilation is a primary concern with any cover, since dead air will quickly increase the humidity level inside a cover. When humidity rises, mildew begins to form, even in a "breathing" material like Acrilan. So make sure that provisions are made to keep fresh air circulating throughout the covered area.

Before selecting a cover maker, take a walk around the docks and study the quality of his covers. They should fit neatly, without being overly loose or tight. There should be a reinforcing of the cloth where it chafes against a sharp object like life-line stanchions or cleats, and there should be extra layers where the snaps or zippers are attached.

At this time, decide what you want in a cover. A one-piece cover for a 25-footer can be awkward to remove and store, and probably should have been made in two or three sections. Think out where you want access to the boat. For example, there should be a provision for entering the cockpit of the boat without unsnapping the entire cover. A cover can often be made that incorporates the sunshade or cockpit awning, thus cutting your canvas costs.

Cover makers point out that many boatowners don't recognize the real value of a cover. A good cover on a fiberglass boat will pay for itself in about three years just in the reduction of maintenance and repairs needed. So don't overlook the cover as a protection for your investment. All in all, a good cover can add a large chunk of value to your boat at resale time. And it will make your boating easier by keeping the boat clean and ready to go at a moment's notice.

8

~·~·~·~·~·~·

Engines

A few years ago, most boats the size of a trailerable sailboat didn't have engines. It was assumed that the skipper could maneuver the boat through any weather and any waterway under sail alone. Fortunately, that macho attitude has been tempered by time as well as the realities of getting in and out of marinas that are now crowded. So you'll want an engine for your boat.

You have several choices. If you're buying a new boat, the dealer probably handles at least one line of outboard motors and will try to encourage you to buy that engine with your boat. Depending on the price, it may or may not be a good deal. As with everything else, it's wise to shop price. Runabout dealers may offer good discounts on the small-horsepower outboards that they don't want to stock, and you may find good prices at sporting-goods or fishing-equipment stores since the motors will be in the small sizes.

In general, you'll probably be interested in an outboard of between 5 and 10 hp. For the most part, outboards in this power range are about the same size and weight, so you should seriously consider getting the larger motor.

The initial cost is the one drawback, but you may save enough in operating costs to cancel that out over a period of a couple of years. A larger outboard will push your boat, for example, at 5 knots while running at half throttle, though a small outboard has to use full power to hold the same speed. The fuel economy will be better with the large engine at half throttle, plus you'll be wearing the parts less.

A second bonus to buying a larger outboard is that you will probably have extra equipment, such as full shifting, an alternator for electrical power, or electric starting.

You'll want full gearshift, which is forward, neutral, and reverse, because it makes boat handling far simpler. If you don't have shifting, you have to stop and start the engine when docking and you may not be able to back up if your motor mount doesn't allow the engine to swivel in a full circle.

The most popular mounting method for outboards in trailerable sailboats is a bracket on the stern. This isn't the most convenient method, since the outboard is hard to reach for controlling the speed and shifting, and it's also unprotected from the elements. Some trailerables have outboard wells in the stern locker through which the engine protrudes with the drawback that this is yet another hole in your hull. But the engine is protected and can be locked away by closing the hatch.

With the stern motor mount, you'll need a longshaft outboard. This is a standard engine with a spacer that lengthens the lower unit so that the propeller reaches the water. Be sure that the engine doesn't just reach the water, but is deep enough so that it won't pop out every time you go over a swell. That's annoying as well as hard on the engine.

Try to find an outboard that has a separate gas tank rather than a built-in tank. It's easier to refill if you can take the tank to the fuel pump rather than trying to pour from a small can into the outboard, and the separate tank will hold more to give you more cruising range. Most small outboards have provisions for adding separate tanks even if they aren't included in the base price.

Take a look at the actual weight and size of the outboard before you buy it. You'll be lifting this motor on a regular basis, and you need to store it someplace in the boat. Make sure you can handle it and store it before you commit yourself to purchasing it. If possible, take the outboard to the boat and see if it will fit into your storage area—sometimes a small protrusion will keep an otherwise small outboard from fitting.

Try to find an engine that has an underwater exhaust, particularly if you have an outboard well. The smoke and fumes will be buried in the prop wash and won't surface until they are far astern, which will make everyone happier.

The major outboard manufacturers offer several propeller choices, and you should opt for the so-called "power prop," if offered. This is usually a three-bladed prop instead of the standard two-bladed one, and it will get a better "bite" on the water and push your boat more easily than the two-bladed speed prop sold to fishermen. Some manufacturers, such as Evinrude and Johnson, offer two outboards based on the same engine: one for rowboats and one for sailboats. The sailing version has

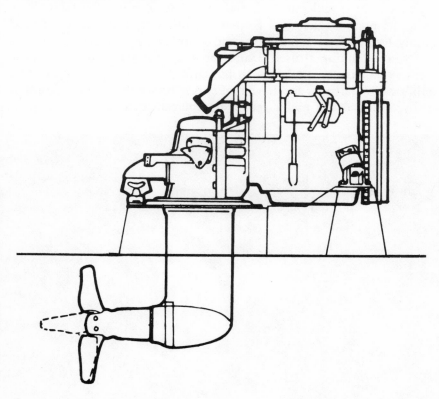

Installation drawing of a Volvo Penta "sail-drive" engine showing the compact engine as well as the outboard-type through-hull lower unit and folding propeller.

a different propeller and a lower gear ratio to move heavier loads.

One innovation in engines is the "sail-drive." It is an inboard engine based on outboard motor parts. It installs permanently inside the boat, but it uses the powerhead from a small outboard and, instead of a conventional prop shaft, it uses an outboardlike lower unit that protrudes through the hull. The sail-drive offers the convenience of inboard power (electric start, engine controls, shifting, built-in fuel tank) with the simplicity of the outboard engine, which can be repaired readily. The installation is simple, even in older boats, since the engine mount is delivered with the engine and you simply glass it into place. The engine weight is still minimal, and the OMC Zephyr, for example, is 15 hp, 95 pounds, has up to a 40-amp alternator, and can be repaired by any Evinrude or Johnson service shop.

If you're looking at used boats, you should move cautiously in the engine area. Your best bet is to have the engine taken to a factory-authorized repairman and have him check it over thoroughly. It might save you the cost of major repair or replacement later.

Be sure to check the outboard serial number and identification code so that you'll know what year and which options were originally included. Have the serial number listed on your purchase offer, too.

This picture of the lower unit of an outboard engine on a used trailerable sailboat is an example of what to watch out for when buying a used engine. The pockmarks indicate that the engine has been left in salt water, and there may have been a deterioration of the metal or other problems from such neglect.

Your first step in your own survey is to make a visual check. Remove the engine cover and look at the overall condition. If there is extensive corrosion on the unpainted surfaces, it indicates that someone hasn't taken good care of the outboard. Discolored paint around the spark-plug holes on the head is probably caused by overheating, which may have caused unseen internal problems as well.

While the engine cover is off, check the identification plate, which will give a serial number and model number. Copy the numbers down, and make sure they appear on your purchase paperwork as well. All outboards use a coding system to determine year and horsepower rating. If you have any questions, ask a dealer to tell you what the numbers mean. The code will also indicate whether it was originally a longshaft model or if this was added later, possibly by an owner without the proper tools or instructions. Use the code for your own protection.

When testing an outboard, make sure that the engine is cold when you try to start it. It should catch immediately and settle down to a smooth idle within a few minutes. If the seller has warmed the engine for you, he may be trying to hide something.

Check the oil dipstick. The oil should be dark and show no evidence of water contamination. Dirty or low oil indicates poor maintenance, as do oil leaks around the lower unit or out of the prop shaft. These seals can be expensive to replace.

Check the condition of the electrical wiring, spark-plug wires, and other electrical accessories. Look also at the rubber hoses and fuel lines to see if they are cracked or deteriorated.

At the very least, have the engine used on your demo sail and see how well it operates. If you have any questions (and even if you haven't), ask to see the service history. The owner should have kept his repair records and bills, which will indicate how regularly he had the engine tuned and checked, plus any major repairs.

One big mistake that trailerable sailboat owners make is buying an outboard that is too small for their needs. Just because an engine can push your boat at 5 knots in a quiet harbor doesn't mean that it can shove the boat against a current or into waves when you really need the engine. Buy more power than you need, and you'll never regret it.

9

Galley Gear

The reaction of most women to the galley found on the trailerable sailboat is first hysterical laughter and then "Oh, my god, you aren't kidding." You certainly won't have the space you're used to at home, but you'll have everything you need.

Your major galley decision will probably be the stove, and there are a variety of styles available. Ask any boatman what kind of stove fuel he uses and you're certain to have your ear bent. Few topics generate such heat! Even worse, most dockside statements bear little resemblance to fact. Each type of stove fuel has good and bad points, so check carefully before choosing.

Alcohol is the most common stove fuel, and alcohol stoves are installed as standard equipment on most trailerables. Alcohol is a liquid fuel, which means that it is bought in a stoppered jug just like moonshine and poured into the stove tank.

The primary recommendations for alcohol stoves are that the fire can be extinguished by water and that it is a clean fuel (referring to the amount of soot or smoke that can discolor your ceiling).

On the other hand, alcohol doesn't produce much heat compared to other fuels, and it takes a long time to make a pot of coffee. Alcohol is expensive (as much as good rum in some areas!), and it's hard to find

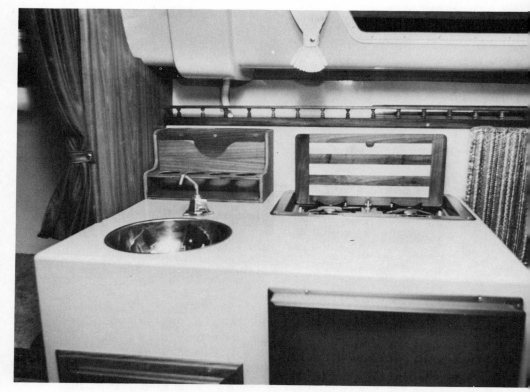

This trailerable has a stove mounted far back on the counter, which (1) isn't convenient and (2) places the flame close to the curtains overhead. There are good counter space and storage racks, but the icebox is side-opening (below the counter) and there are no rails around the counter to keep food and utensils from sliding off.

in foreign countries. Most modern alcohol stoves are pressurized, which means that you have to use a hand pump to put the fuel under pressure prior to each usage.

Alcohol is also one of the more difficult fuels to ignite, because the liquid has to be vaporized before ignition. A primer cup under the burner is lit, which preheats the vaporizer in each burner, and, when the prime is burned off, the burner can be lit. This process is one drawback, since you can create a spectacular flare-up during the process.

Because of the small burner, alcohol stoves generally have unsatisfactory ovens, ones that cause hot spots and uneven baking. In addition, during the course of meal preparation, you may have to pump up the tank again, which will cause a change in the flame temperature.

Many sailors find that the sickly sweet smell of alcohol makes them seasick. There is no real solution to this except to stay outside the cabin.

Although the alcohol stove is the most likely to be used aboard trailerables, it's worth a quick overview of other fuels and their features.

Kerosene is a sister fuel to alcohol, and is called paraffin in foreign boating magazines. It is hotter than alcohol, but it also will soot up the cabin. It's available worldwide, but it also smells and cannot be extinguished with water. It needs alcohol for a primer, so you have to carry both fuels anyway.

Electricity is perhaps the simplest fuel, but you'd need a long extension cord since the trailerable sailboat is too small for a generator. One solution worth exploring, however, is a combination alcohol and electric stove. It gives simple cooking at dockside or on the trailer (as long as you're near an electrical plug) and alcohol cooking while under way.

From the above-mentioned "simple" fuels, the next step for the boatman is to install a pressure system of either liquid petroleum gas (LPG) or compressed natural gas (CNG).

LPG is the most common of the pressurized fuels, and its two main types are propane and butane. Under pressure, the gas turns to liquid, so a considerable amount can be stored in a fairly small tank. Released from pressure, it regassifies and burns on a stove much like the one in your home.

Butane is sometimes called the cook's delight because it has few of the bad habits of alcohol. It requires no priming, regulates well, and the oven heats evenly.

But there's always a catch. With LPG, the gas is heavier than air and quite explosive. A leaking fuel line will allow gas to accumulate in the bilge of your boat just like gasoline fumes and can produce a stupendous explosion if ignited by a spark.

On the positive side, LPG is cheap, burns cleanly, requires little maintenance, and is odorless. LPG is banned by the Coast Guard for use on charter boats because they consider it dangerous, but many yachtsmen are perfectly happy with their LPG units.

CNG is a newcomer to the stove market, and it's the same fuel that is used in your home. It has all the positive properties of LPG: easy to light, clean-burning, odorless, and provides an even heat. Best of all, CNG is lighter than air so leaks are easily vented. The only drawbacks to CNG at this time are limited availability in some parts of the country and a higher cost than LPG.

Since the installation and initial cost of most stoves other than alcohol rule them out for trailerable sailboats, a word on installation and use of alcohol stoves might be useful.

Clean the stove at least once a season and more often if you use it often. Disassemble the burners, remove the carbon deposits, and you'll be surprised at how well the stove operates. The packing glands on the tank and burners should be lubricated often because alcohol dries them out.

When you're lighting the stove, use long wooden matches for two reasons: to keep your hands out of the way and because paper matches can soak up stove fuel.

Be sure the stove is mounted securely, or, if it is intended to be moved, make certain that it can be held firmly while in use. The best place for a stove is where there is ventilation, but without enough wind to blow the flame out. If it has to be used close to a bulkhead, cover the nearby area with metal-sheathed asbestos and don't let your curtains hang over the stove area.

Every stove that you use while under way should have sea rails or clamps to hold pots and pans firmly on the burner and prevent any sudden motion from flipping hot food onto the cook.

Some safety precautions seem basic, but don't forget that flames consume oxygen, so don't cook in a closed cabin; and never leave the stove untended.

One useful accessory for your boat is a gimbaled Sea Swing stove. It's perfect for that hot cup of soup on a chilly afternoon. It isn't good for all cooking purposes, but it's a lot simpler than using the regular stove.

The second most important item to consider is the icebox. While many trailerable sailboats have an icebox built into the galley area, others leave it to your own ingenuity to figure out how to keep your beer cold. If you don't have an icebox, you'll need to add one.

The easiest method is simply to purchase an ice chest from a sporting-goods store. Two types are available: a low-priced version made of

This trailerable doesn't earn many points with the layout. The stove simply sits on top of the cabinet and has no place to be stored. The icebox is side-opening, which wastes cold air and allows food to fall out. The electrical panel, on the lower side of the starboard settee, is placed where the switches can be accidentally flipped on or off with the foot.

foam and a tougher chest made of unbreakable polyethylene, which is what you'll want. Beware of all metal fittings, since they are apt to rust in a marine environment. Pick the biggest chest that you can fit aboard your boat without infringing on living space. A good camp ice chest is actually better than most built-in iceboxes because it will have better insulation, it's easier to clean, and it can be used away from the boat for other trips.

If your trailerable has an icebox built in, then you won't have much choice. For your consideration, however, there are some things you should know. A top-opening icebox is best for two reasons: the cold air won't spill out every time you open it, and the contents won't fall out when the boat heels over in a breeze.

The insulation on a built-in icebox probably won't be enough, but it should be at least two inches thick on *all* sides, including the lid. Insulation works in direct proportion to thickness, so a four-inch layer of insulation will keep your foods twice as long as a two inch-layer.

Every icebox should have dividers or compartments to keep food separated and accessible, but your chances of finding that are almost nonexistent. Plan to add them yourself. The icebox should have a drain to eliminate melted ice water, since ice melts faster if it is sitting in water. Make sure that the drain doesn't flow into the bilge of the boat, but into either a separate sump or overboard through a sink drain. If the melted ice water drains into the bilge, it will carry along tiny food particles that will then rot and smell up the bilge. At the same time, check to make sure that the drain has an S curve that will hold water and prevent cold air from draining along with the water.

If you find that your water has a bad taste as it comes from the tank, you can reduce the taste by replacing the plumbing with taste-free hose. You can also soak the tank in a potion such as vinegar and water (for fiberglass taste) or baking soda and water (for flat water). You can even try adding a water filter to cut the flavor, but you'll probably always have it. It's a fact of boating life. For that reason, a lot of families carry plastic jugs of water, which can be purchased once and then refilled at home.

Regardless of whether you plan to drink the water from the boat or not, make sure that the water tank is accessible. It should have a removable plate so that you can reach in and give it a good scrubbing occasionally. A cool, dark water tank, especially when almost empty, is a fine breeding ground for bacteria, so keep your tank filled and be prepared to clean it. If you have to leave it for long periods, add a little chlorine to the tank for protection.

In all likelihood, the tank won't be sufficient for long periods of cruising, so you'll have to decide whether to add an additional tank with its plumbing or simply to rely on finding water wherever you cruise.

One way to conserve fresh water is to install a salt-water pump at the sink. This draws water from outside the boat that can be used for the initial washing of dishes or other uses that don't require pure water.

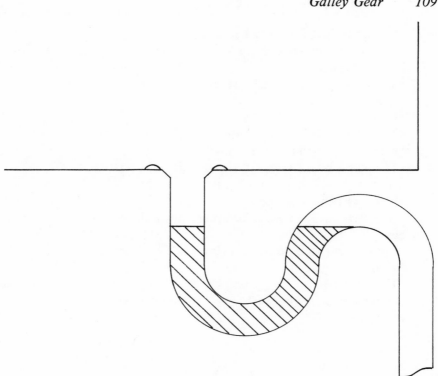

A cutaway of the icebox drain showing the S curve that stays filled with water to prevent the cold air from draining through the empty pipe.

Once you've done the first washing, rinse the dishes with fresh water and you'll cut your water needs considerably.

Many families use their household utensils and equipment aboard their boat, while others prefer to have a separate set for the boat. If you use the household utensils, be sure you have a good checklist. There's nothing worse than finding yourself at a deserted cove with an evening meal to prepare and no can opener.

The following is a starting point which can be modified up or down to suit your needs:

· Knives: paring, utility, meat slicing (all with blade covers)

· Spoons: slotted spoon for serving, large and medium kitchen spoons, plastic or wood spoon for nonstick pans

· Long-handled fork and spatula
· At least two can openers, bottle-cap remover, corkscrew, and two beer-can openers
· Skillet, large and small pot, all with covers
· Tea kettle
· Coffee pot
· Tableware, dishes, mugs for a number of guests
· Measuring spoons, measuring cup
· Chopping board (even if one is built in)
· Nested plastic bowls with lids
· Salt and pepper shakers
· Asbestos burner pad, sink brush, pot holders, ice pick, ice tote bag
· Funnel, garbage bags, scouring pads (bronze, not steel, which rusts)
· Thermos bottle
· Other items: sewing kit, Lysol, notepaper, and pencils

10

~~~~~~~~~~

Electronics

There are some who claim that since Columbus made it all the way without electronics, there's no need to put money into modern equipment. They also seem to forget that Columbus was lost.

There are thousands of different types of "black boxes" available in the marine marketplace, ranging from simple radios to satellite navigation systems. But the trailerable sailboat owner can focus on a smaller area. Electronics that he should consider include (in no order) the VHF and CB radios, radio direction finder, depth sounder, and speed instruments.

In general, there are three basics to keep in mind when you buy electronics. First, make sure there is a suitable warranty on the product that covers the uses you intend it for. Some units, for example, may not be intended for exposure to salt air or dampness.

Second, try to buy a product that has a local parts and service outlet. In most cases, this will be the marine electronics dealer, but in some instances you may get a better price from a mail-order catalogue store. Before you send off your check, find out who repairs the product locally.

Last, make sure that the product is intended for (or at least suitable to) the marine environment. This is particularly true with CB radios aimed at the automobile market and which have components that will rust.

VHF RADIOS. The VHF (very high frequency) radio is the basic two-way communication tool in boating. In optimum conditions it will reach 40 to 50 miles, although 20 to 30 miles is a better everyday range. Since the radio waves travel in a straight line, VHF radios won't transmit over or around mountains, and reception to shore stations will depend almost entirely on the height of the receiving antenna. On the West Coast, where shore stations are on mountaintops, reception is good over long distances. But the Gulf and eastern coasts have considerably shorter ranges.

There are two types of VHF radios: the crystal radio and the synthesized set. The basic unit is the crystal radio, with a pair of crystals (sending and receiving) for each channel. Since two channels are required by law for emergencies (6 and 16), that leaves ten channels for your own uses. If you're looking for a low-cost radio primarily for emergency use, the basic set will meet your needs. Prices start at around $300, and crystals are $15 to $30 per pair.

With those costs in mind, you can often purchase a synthesized VHF radio for as little as $100 more than a basic crystal set. The synthesized radio does not use crystals and generally offers either 55 or 78 channels, all of which are included. The synthesized radio gives you a larger choice of ship-to-ship channels as well as more ship-to-shore channels for use in areas with considerable radio traffic that may tie up the popular channels.

When deciding between the radios, be sure to compare the total price for each set with installation and antenna. Often, a package deal from a marine electronics store, including the antenna, cable, installation, and certification, will be only a few dollars more than you'd pay for the basic unit.

Give serious consideration to the antenna you purchase, since it is a key element in the quality of your radio reception and transmission. A 3db antenna is the most common on small sailboats, and the best place for it is at the top of your mast to increase your range. This will involve connectors so that you can lower and trailer your mast, but the electronics technician can handle that for you. You should also consider spending a few extra dollars for an oversized cable with foam insulation, especially if you plan a masthead mount.

You may not need it for local voyages, but if you intend to do any distance cruising away from popular areas you probably should buy a spare antenna that can plug into the back of your radio in case you are dismasted and need to call for assistance.

In general, most radios produce the FCC-allowable maximum of 25 watts of power, although some less expensive sets are rated at only 10 to 12 watts. Get the most power for your dollar.

RDFS. Second only to a chart as an important navigational tool, the radio direction finder (RDF) is used to locate your position by triangulation between radio beacons. It can also be used to home in on a particular harbor that has a beacon, and it is an essential piece of equipment for anyone venturing outside the harbor entrance.

An RDF is a sensitive radio receiver with a directional antenna, which, when turned, will indicate the direction of a particular radio beacon that is marked on your charts.

There are three types of RDF units to consider, although a fourth type is the automatic direction finder, which is too expensive for most trailerables.

The simplest RDF is the unit that looks like a portable radio and that has a rotating antenna on top. It often picks up several different radio

The two most popular styles of RDF for the trailerable sailboat are the upright version (left) and the compact unit (right). Each has the directional antenna on the top, both have null meters, and the upright style usually has more radio bands.

bands in addition to the beacon band, and is fine for occasional use.

The most common RDF is a larger unit, usually flat for stability, that again has the rotating antenna on the top and fewer nonessential bands.

The last type is the hand-held RDF, which resembles a pistol and is pointed at the horizon until a meter indicates the direction of the radio beacon. This is a good unit for sailboats, since you can stand at the rail away from the disruptive influences of the mast and the metal rigging.

All portable RDF units operate on their own batteries, usually six or eight flashlight batteries. As a minimum, the RDF should receive the beacon band, which runs from 190 to 550 kilohertz. The ability to pick up the AM broadcast band (550–1600 kHz) is also useful since you can home in on these stations when you're out of range for some radio beacons. Any other bands, such as FM or shortwave, are simply icing on the cake and are there only for entertainment value.

RDF prices start at about $150 for the upright models, and there are some specific considerations to take into account before you buy. Check the advertised bearing accuracy, which will govern how accurate your navigation is, and reject any units that don't have at least $\pm$ 5°. It's worth the extra dollars to buy a unit that has a sense antenna to determine from which direction the radio signal is coming. This will prevent you from heading directly away from a beacon while thinking that you're going toward it. Digital tuning is useful for finding radio beacons that are close together in frequency. A large null meter makes the direction-finding procedure easier, as does a well-lit dial face. When testing an RDF, be sure to tune in to a radio beacon and not to a broadcast radio station. Even five-dollar throwaway radios sound good when tuned to a 100,000-watt rock station. Listen to see how clearly the RDF picks up the beacon code and how strongly the null is indicated on the dial.

SOUNDERS. Since you have bought a trailerable sailboat at least in part for its ability to sail in shallow waters, a depth sounder is a useful addition to see how shallow the water is really getting. A depth sounder sends ultrasonic pulses toward the bottom and measures the time it takes for them to reflect back. This is then displayed in different ways, and the primary decisions in purchasing a sounder are on the display style and the depth range.

The simplest display is digital, and it prints out the depth in either feet or fathoms. Next in simplicity is the dial-face analog display that is like a clockface with a needle pointing at the appropriate depth.

The most popular display and the most useful is the rotating flasher. A small bulb, preferably a light-emitting diode (LED), is on the edge of a spinning disc, and it flashes at the number marking the depth. The flasher display will indicate the depth as well as the type of bottom (to an experienced watcher) and schools of fish at different levels. The last type, and least suitable for trailerables, is the recording sounder, which graphs the bottom.

The transducer, which sends the sonic pulses, can be installed in three ways: on the hull bottom, in a box inside, or as a removable unit. The traditional method has been to drill a hole in the bottom and bolt the transducer through the hull. This is the simplest method, although care must be taken to make sure that it is positioned vertically. It should also be faired in to minimize drag, and it should be located away from trailer rollers or pads.

A recent development for fiberglass boats is to mount the transducer in a watertight box inside the hull. When the box is filled with water, the pulses pass right through the fiberglass hull and you have accurate soundings without an outside transducer. Most digital sounders won't work with this method, and this method won't work on hulls that have a core material or air bubbles in the fiberglass. To see if your boat is suitable for a box mount, fill a plastic bag with water and place the transducer inside it. Wet the plastic bag and put it against the hull in the spot you've selected. If the sounder works adequately, try moving the boat to deeper water and see if it continues to respond normally. If so, you've found your spot. If not, try the bag in other spots. You'll lose a little of your precious storage with a box, but you'll be cutting drag. It's your choice.

The last mounting method is offered by many manufacturers on their shallow-water sounders, and it is a removable bracket for the transom. You'll still have to route the wiring, but you won't have to bother with boxes or holes.

Whichever style you choose, get some advice from a dealer before you install the sounder, because it should be kept away from the keel, which can cause reflections that make the sounder inaccurate.

When looking for a sounder, be sure that it is visible in bright sunlight. Older flashers, for example, had neon lights that could barely be seen in daylight. Flashers should also have a sensitivity control to

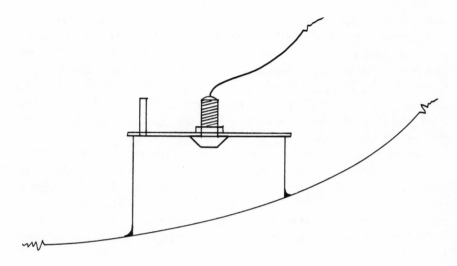

A side-view drawing of a depth-sounder transducer mounted in a box inside a fiberglass hull. The box is fiberglassed to the hull and filled with water through the spout at the top left. The top plate can be unscrewed for access to the transducer. A small amount of oil should be added to the water to form a layer that will prevent evaporation.

fine-tune them. More and more sounders are incorporating depth alarms that ring when you reach a certain depth, say 15 feet, and alert you that the water is shallow. They can also be used when you are anchored to warn you that your anchor has dragged and you are drifting into shallow water. Don't forget to allow for tidal change or you'll be awakened at low tide.

Depending on your primary sailing areas and your planned use of your trailerable sailboat, you may want to choose a 60-foot sounder or a combination 60-foot/60-fathom unit that reaches 360 feet on the fathom scale. If you plan to do a lot of sailing in shallow areas, you'd be better off with a low-range sounder that is accurate in small numbers. A 100-foot sounder is harder to read in small increments than a 25-foot sounder. Don't consider any sounder that doesn't advertise at least a 5-percent accuracy level.

CB RADIO. Citizens Band radio has, for better or worse, entered the marine field when the Coast Guard announced that they will monitor

CB in certain boating areas. CB has long been the Wailing Wall of this country, where you can hear everything from the "breaker, breaker" of truckdrivers to drug shipments being dropped off. With 100,000 CB radios being registered every month in 1979 (not counting illegal sets), there are more than enough idiots on the air.

On the positive side, however, CB does provide an excellent two-way communication system at a reasonable price, particularly for inland waterways where no VHF equipment is in use. CB does not have any facilities for ship-to-shore telephone hookups like VHF, but it will give you an emergency radio where you can be sure to reach someone in most parts of the country. It can also give you information on where the fish are biting, whether a cove is crowded, or what the weather at the other end of the lake is like.

With a working range of 15 to 20 miles and an FCC imposed limit of 150 miles, there is always the possibility of skip, an atmospheric phenomenon that sometimes allows contact over thousands of miles while preventing contact within a few miles.

When looking for a CB radio, check to see if it is intended for marine use or whether it's designed for the cab of a big Fruehauf truck. The same is particularly true of the antenna, because an automotive antenna won't work on a boat since it has no ground.

The maximum power of CBs is 4 watts, and you should get all of it. Most modern CBs are 23-channel, and solid-state construction uses 12v DC current. Be sure to see that there is an FCC-type acceptance stamp on the radio or you won't be legal. Prices for CB radios are hovering around $100, although you can often find good buys as dealers unload sets that haven't sold.

INSTRUMENTS. Probably the most useful instrument aboard a trailerable sailboat is a good speedometer. Other items, like wind-speed and wind-direction indicators are frills unless you're really a serious racer. But a speedometer can provide you with a navigational tool, and, if equipped with a log to record miles traveled, it can simplify your dead reckoning of where you are.

Speedometers come in all shapes and sizes, starting at $25 for a simple unit and working up to several hundred dollars. A basic speedo with a dial or digital display and the ability to add a log later is good for a new boatowner.

The underwater sensor is usually one of three types: a wand, a paddle, or a pitot tube. They all will foul on seaweed—there is no ideal solution to this problem. The wand and the pitot tube usually require an outside power source, while the paddlewheel version produces its own current in case you don't want to use your battery. They all need outside electricity for the dial light, however.

While it might be nice to shock your friends with a 25-mph speedometer, you're better off choosing one about one-third faster than your actual top speed. If you expect to reach 9 knots in your trailerable, then a 12-knot speedometer is plenty.

Be sure to install the underwater sensor where it won't be broken during trailer launching, and make sure that replacement parts are readily available. You'll always need them.

11

~.~.~.~.~.~.

Safety Equipment

Safety equipment is a broad-ranging topic since, theoretically, anything that makes your boating safer should be included. But for the purpose of this chapter, we'll look only at those specific safety items that are either required by law or strongly recommended.

As a starting point when you are outfitting your boat, contact the nearest Coast Guard office and ask it to send you a copy of CG–290, "Federal Requirements for Recreational Boats." This spells out all the legal requirements that you need to meet and, since they change often, check the most current information.

What were once called life jackets are now known as Personal Flotation Devices (PFDs), and any that you buy must carry the Coast Guard stamp of approval. All boats larger than 16 feet must have at least one PFD for every person on board as well as one throwable PFD in case someone falls into the water. PFDs come in several different styles, but those most commonly used on trailerable sailboats are the "Mae West"-type life vests. Coats that meet Coast Guard standards can also count toward the legal minimum, and some skippers use the "float coat" as a simple solution to carrying PFDs. The throwable PFD can be a conventional life ring, but it makes more sense aboard a trailerable sailboat to use a square life cushion that can also serve as a cockpit backrest.

Be wary, though: PFDs must be of an appropriate size for the persons who intend to wear them. If you carry five adult PFDs but you are stopped when you have only one adult and four children aboard, you'll probably get a citation. So carry extra PFDs to fit your changing crew needs. PFDs are one area where it isn't wise to skimp. If you don't have a PFD when you need one, you may not have to worry about PFDs again.

If your boat is equipped with a motor, then it must meet the fire-extinguisher requirements. For boats of less than 26 feet in length, at least one class B-1 extinguisher must be aboard. Boats over 26 feet may carry either two B-1 or one B-2 extinguishers.

Like PFDs, the minimal expense of extra fire extinguishers is the cheapest insurance you can buy. Even if you have no engine aboard but do have a stove, you should have a fire extinguisher. Mount the fire extinguishers where they can be reached in case of fire. Don't put them in the area of a potential fire. One extinguisher in the galley area, one under a cockpit seat hatch, and one near the forward bunks make for a good start.

Boats less than 26 feet must have a whistle or horn that is audible for at least a half mile. A compressed-air horn is the usual solution, although a mouth horn is a good backup.

Boats of 26 feet and larger must also carry a bell for use in fog. The requirements change again at 40 feet. But since there aren't many trailerable 40-foot sailboats, we'll leave that area alone.

The above items are legally required, and should be used only as a starting point. The U.S. Coast Guard Auxiliary offers a free boat examination to qualify for their Courtesy Motorboat Decal, and their list of equipment is useful in fitting out. They have added some items and beefed up the requirements on some legal gear. The exam is open to all boats, and you will not be cited if you fail. It's strictly a way to help boatmen outfit their boats properly.

The Auxiliary list requires one PFD per bunk, rather than for each person, which is a reasonable assumption. They require additional fire extinguishers beyond the legal minimum, and they must be located for easy access in an emergency. They require distress signaling equipment, such as flares, dye markers, smoke flares, and orange flags. Anchor and line are also needed to receive the decal.

On the Auxiliary recommended list is a second anchor, a bilge pump, dock lines, a boat hook, a flash or spotlight, plus acceptable installations of boat gear such as the stove and fuel tank.

Looking at the items individually, choose the kind of PFD that is going to be most useful aboard your boat. If your family needs jackets, combine the law with a flotation coat, but be sure your crew takes them aboard every trip. If you add extra life jackets, make sure they are readily accessible. A plastic laundry tub under the cockpit will keep the PFDs clean, dry, and accessible.

Once you've met the fire-extinguisher requirement, make sure that everyone aboard knows how to use them. Go over how to remove them from the bracket, how to use the trigger, and how to aim at the base of the fire with a sweeping motion. The best fire extinguisher used incorrectly won't put out a wastebasket fire. It's worth the refill charge to actually discharge one extinguisher to see how it works. You should recharge the extinguishers each spring, and that's a good time to try them out.

Running lights are usually factory-installed, but have them checked for legality in your waters by the Coast Guard or the Coast Guard Auxiliary. At the time of this writing, the laws are in a state of flux between the International and the Inland rules, so make sure that you are legal for your planned waters.

The techniques of anchoring the trailerable sailboat will be covered later, but for now you should make sure that you have proper anchor gear. There is so much difference of opinion about types of anchors that you may have to rely on local advice on what works in your area. Some anchors work best in grassy bottoms, others in sand, others in mud or rock. Where you plan to anchor will determine which anchor you choose. The same rule applies to the length of your anchor line or rode, as it's called. The rode should be a synthetic like nylon with good stretch characteristics to absorb shocks, and it should be at least ten times the depth of the water that you plan to anchor in. If you normally anchor in 25 feet of water, have at least 250 feet of anchor rode plus a short length of chain at the anchor end. For trailerable sailboats of 25 feet, a 6-foot length of chain is plenty.

Take care in how the anchor, chain, and rode are joined. The most common method is to shackle the chain to the anchor, splice an eye

The anchor line is spliced to a thimble, through which a shackle attaches the chain. Be sure that the shackle is seized with wire to prevent it from unscrewing. A similarly seized shackle joins the anchor to the chain.

with a protective thimble into the rode, and then shackle the rode to the chain. Both shackles should be secured with wire to keep them from unscrewing by accident.

Using examples set by Danforth for its lightweight anchors, a 25-foot sailboat anchoring in 15 feet of water should carry an 8-pound Danforth with 150 feet of ⅜-inch nylon and 3 feet of chain as a working anchor. For a second anchor or as a lunch hook for short stops, Danforth suggests a 4-pound Danforth with 100 feet of ¼-inch nylon.

One important item is a bilge pump, although it has often been said that "nothing is as effective as a frightened man with a bucket." Nevertheless, a permanently mounted bilge pump, accessible from the cockpit, is an important safety item. Be sure that it reaches the deepest part of the boat, and that there is a protective screen to keep it from clogging on debris floating in the bilge.

Distress signaling equipment was once left to the boatowner's discretion, but in 1981 the U.S. Coast Guard implemented new rules that dictate the type and quantity of signals that must be carried by all boats. Distress signals for both day and night use are required, and the buyer can choose from several types of signals, including hand-held smoke or

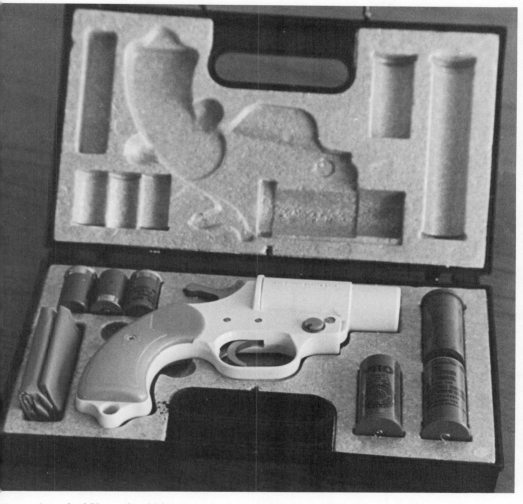

A typical Very pistol kit comes in a watertight case and includes the pistol and several different day and night flares.

red flares, Very pistols that shoot parachute flares, electric SOS lights, and distress flags. All varieties are available in marine hardware stores, including some prepackaged kits that are watertight and include the legal minimums. One word of caution: don't ever use highway flares aboard your boat because they are both dangerous and illegal.

A compass is both a safety item and a navigational tool. Pick a good compass, have it corrected so that the metal aboard your boat doesn't affect it, and store it in a safe place. Combined with a local chart, your compass will get you home safely.

Other gear that can be considered safety equipment includes dock lines long enough to be used for towing, a first-aid kit (see Appendix), a paddle if your boat is of a size that can be moved in calm water by paddling, spare parts and tools (see Appendix), and navigational equipment.

SECTION III

The Trailer

12

~~~~~~~~

Buying Tips

Many buyers spend months comparing boats and dealers and then, having selected their boat, take only a few moments to choose the trailer. Too often, this leads to a boating experience that isn't much fun because the boat is hard to tow or hard to launch or hard to retrieve.

A good trailer is also important to your boat's health, because the trailerable sailboat will probably spend 80 percent of its life on the trailer. No boat is designed to sit on a trailer, and the best support for any boat is in the water, where it is uniformly and evenly held. A good trailer should duplicate the support of water as closely as possible, particularly since a boat will undergo greater shocks on the trailer than in the water.

When looking for a trailer, there are four basic considerations. The trailer should support the weight and the shape of the boat uniformly. It should provide a safe cradle for the boat on the road. It should be easy to handle during launching and loading. And it should be easy to maintain. Any trailer that doesn't meet those requirements is going to be irritating at best and dangerous at worst.

The biggest mistake trailer buyers make, according to most trailer manufacturers, is to buy a trailer of the wrong capacity. Every trailer is designed to carry a specific weight range, and anything outside that range is wrong. If you buy a trailer that is for a smaller weight than your boat, you're liable to have a failure of the chassis or suspension. If, on the other hand, you decide to play it safe and "overbuy" a trailer, you may damage your boat since the heavier-duty trailer will transmit all the shocks to the boat rather than absorb them. The moral: buy a trailer that matches your boat.

How do you determine your capacity needs? Start with the weight of your boat, which is probably listed in the advertising brochures. Check with the dealer to make sure that the weight is correct. Add to that all the items that you'll either install on the boat or put aboard during the trip to the water. Don't forget the outboard and its fuel tank (gasoline is about 7 pounds per gallon), food, water, clothing, sails, anchor, dinghy, and miscellaneous gear. It isn't hard to increase the boats bare weight by half a ton with all your possessions. That's the number you want to give the trailer manufacturer. Don't add in a safety factor because he's already done it.

Once you've decided on a capacity, you'll need to start looking at trailers the same way you looked at boats. Start with construction. A trailer for boats the size we're discussing should be made of heavy-duty structural channel steel. Aluminum is fine for saving weight on light boats, but not for big sailboats. Maximum strength is achieved by bending the cross frames to shape rather than welding several pieces of steel together. Check the welds to see how they look. A good weld will be smoothly rippled for the length of the joint. There should be no gaps, cracks, or protrusions coming from the weld.

The trailer should be undercoated with a rust-inhibiting primer before the final white paint job. Check with the manufacturer to see if it was. An uncoated trailer will start rusting almost immediately.

The trailer should have fenders to keep rocks from chipping your hull, and the fenders should be bolted on (rather than welded) for easier replacement if damaged. There should be ample step pads around the fenders and in any other areas where you may need to climb up during launching.

You'll need brakes regardless of how light you think your boat is going to be. In most states, brakes are required for any load over 3,000 pounds, and you'll easily be over that minimum.

There are three types of braking systems for trailers in this size range: hydraulic, electric, and surge or inertia. The most popular by far are surge brakes, since they require no modification of the tow car and, in fact, can be towed by several cars without problems. Hydraulic or electric brakes rely on tapping into either the tow car's hydraulic system or the installation of an electrical sensor in the brake system to trigger electric trailer brakes.

Surge brakes rely on the principle of inertia, so that at the first sign of the tow car slowing down, a moving cylinder actuates the trailer brakes to match the slowing.

In addition, whatever brake system you buy should have a breakaway chain to set the brakes should the trailer hitch fail. The chain is attached to the tow car (it's not the safety chain) and to the trailer brakes so that the trailer will stop automatically.

Beware of two-axle trailers that have brakes on only one axle. They may not have enough stopping power, and you could wear out your car brakes more quickly.

Wheel bearings are the next consideration, and your trailerable must have waterproof bearings of one sort or another. There are several popular brands on the market, and you can usually rely on the ones chosen by the trailer builder. Sealed bearings are usually pressure-filled with grease to keep water from entering and rusting the bearing surfaces.

Lights are the last major consideration to your trailer, and you'll be required to have tail lights as well as marker lights along the side of the trailer. If at all possible, the entire light system should be removable, because electrical equipment and water (even fresh) don't mix comfortably. Removable lights are usually one of two kinds: tail lights mounted on a board that may be removed completely and unplugged from the wiring harness or individual lights that may be unclipped and removed separately. Either way, you're protecting the lights.

The alternative to removable lights is either to opt for the more expensive sealed light units or simply to replace your lights regularly. A word of caution: even sealed lights aren't perfect. When a sealed light that is hot from use (like when you ride the brakes while backing to the water) comes in contact with cold water, it will suck in small amounts of moisture which will eventually destroy even a sealed light. If you have sealed lights, disconnect them and allow them to cool before submersion.

Tires are a point to consider carefully. First, they must be of the proper size. You can check to see the capacity for each tire, which is molded into the sidewall. If the capacity of each tire multiplied by the number of tires doesn't exceed the trailer capacity, you're liable to have trouble. Many manufacturers recommend that you try to use the same size tires and wheels as on your tow car so that you'll have an extra spare, but the result simply isn't worth the effort. You're most likely to have a different bolt pattern on the trailer wheel, the tires are going to be different, and buying a spare tire is often much less expensive. Besides, you'll probably keep your boat and trailer longer than you keep the tow car, so you'll have to go through the whole process again if you want matching tires.

Check to see what size tires are available for that particular trailer, and try to order the largest diameter that you can find. A small tire turns faster to cover the same distance as a large tire, which means increased tire wear and increased wheel-bearing heat and stress. At the same time, don't end up buying an odd-sized tire because you may need to replace it in Podunk on Sunday afternoon.

This may all sound academic to you, since the boat of your dreams is already sitting on a trailer that seems acceptable. At this point, you should find out who ordered the trailer: the dealer or the builder. If the trailer came from the factory, then you're probably getting a sturdy and good-fitting trailer. The dealer, on the other hand, may have chosen a trailer based on who gave the largest discount. It's your money. Don't settle for anything less than a good value.

You'll need some extras that you should order at the same time you choose your trailer to make sure that everything fits properly. You'll need a spare tire of the right size and bolt pattern. You'll need to check your tow-car jack to see if it can handle lifting the trailer. It probably can't. So you'll need a husky jack for that tire change.

You may be offered an extendible trailer tongue, which allows the car to stay farther away from the water and still permits the boat to float free. It's a nice option to have, and it simplifies launching immensely.

A tongue jack is essential if it isn't standard equipment. It permits you to hook up the hitch without straining your back. Keel guides that aim the boat onto the trailer are useful, especially if you don't have a large crew. Some trailer manufacturers have folding ladders that mount to the bow roller platform and allow you to climb gracefully aboard without struggling.

Last, you should consider an electric winch if you value your sac-

A trailer tongue extender allows the car to stay farther away from the water as well as putting the trailer in deeper water for easier launching and retrieving.

roiliac. An electric winch is powered by your car's 12-volt electrical system, and it should match up to the weight of your boat. It should have a remote-control capability, so that you can stand away from the wire cable as the boat is winched onto the trailer. That will keep you from being injured if the wire should pop under the load. An electric winch isn't cheap, but if you'd pay five bucks every time you launch for less effort, then you'll pay for it in no time at all.

13

~·~·~·~·~·~·

The Tow Car

There's no question about it. The trailerable sailboat owner is caught between a rock and a hard spot. As moorings and slips become harder to find, the trailerable becomes a more enticing proposition. But the energy crisis has forced the automobile manufacturers to produce cars that don't lend themselves to towing boats. Is there a solution?

Although the outlook isn't particularly bright, there are still a few new cars that are capable of towing boats of three to four tons. Today's average American car is smaller, lighter, and considerably weaker than its counterpart of even five years ago. And the number of cars that can tow boat-sized loads is growing fewer every year.

What do you need for towing purposes? Basically, you need a powerful engine, because almost all other considerations can be dealt with via bolt-on parts such as springs and shocks. You'll need enough power to tow your boat, say 6,000 pounds worth of it, at the current 55-mph speed limit. But even that isn't enough, because you'll need power to get up hills and for situations where you must pass other cars fairly quickly.

On the 1982 market, there are still full-sized cars that can handle tow loads of 3,500 to 6,000 pounds with engines of 350 cubic inches. If you need to tow more than 6,000 pounds, get the idea of a combination family sedan and tow car out of your mind. You need a truck or van of at least a ¾-ton capacity, equipped with the most powerful V-8 that can be found in the 450-ci range.

In either case, you'll also need to order the heavy-duty towing package from your dealer, since it will cost less than having the individual parts added later. The towing package will usually include a seven-wire electrical harness, larger radiator, heavy-duty suspension, heavier alternator and battery, a transmission oil cooler, a power-steering cooler, and larger wheels and tires. With this package, you're probably ready for any length trip you might want to tackle.

But you don't want to buy a new car just to tow your boat, particularly at current car prices. You still have some options. You may be lucky enough to have a family car that can qualify, with some modifications, as a tow car.

If you have a full-sized sedan or a wagon more than five years old, you're probably set if it has a large V-8 engine. If you don't, give some serious thought to buying a used car for your tow purposes.

One trailer-boat enthusiast recently bought a larger boat and found that his station wagon couldn't quite cut it when it came to towing. When he investigated new cars, it took him several days to recover from the prices. So he decided to rebuild his older station wagon for heavier towing duty. For about $2,500, he had the engine and power train from rear axle to radiator thoroughly gone over. Some parts, like the radiator and the transmission, were switched for heavier-duty units. The engine had the smog controls removed (that's illegal, by the way) for more power, and the suspension was beefed up. Gauges to monitor the engine were added along with oil coolers to prevent overheating. For a reasonable price, he had a car that was mechanically almost new and which could pull his new boat easily. That may be an alternative to consider.

If you have a family car that already fits the tow-car requirements, you should prepare it for its new task. Starting with the engine, you'll need to increase the cooling capacity. A larger radiator is one method, and the addition of engine and transmission oil coolers is another way to prolong the car's life.

A transmission oil cooler, for example, prevents heat buildup and subsequent transmission-fluid breakdown, which can cause the transmission to seize. Most mechanics estimate about 30,000 miles of useful life for a tow car without a trans cooler. For between $50 and $100, you can add a cooler, which is considerably cheaper than a rebuild.

You'll need to give the suspension a complete review. If you have a load-equalizing trailer hitch, you won't have to do as much, but you should still consider adding another leaf to the rear springs, perhaps heavier coil springs, and air-filled shocks. Your tires may need upgrading from a low load range to a higher one (check the sidewalls), and some radial tires can cause sway when towing. If that happens, don't hesitate to switch to a bias-ply tire for easier driving.

The one problem that most trailerable sailboat owners confront sooner or later is overheating the tow car. It usually comes from a long uphill grade or from stop-and-go traffic through cities. You can beat the heat by adding auxiliary electric fans to your radiator to increase the air flow, and a coolant recovery system will prevent the loss of water when the radiator boils over. Summertime heat can cause vapor lock in the fuel lines, and the solution is an electric fuel pump.

It all sounds like a lot of effort, but there is nothing more pleasant than towing a big boat behind a fully prepared car on the way to a distant lake.

14

~~~~~~~~

Trailer Hitches

Hitches are the joint between the trailer and the tow car. The wrong hitch can bring disastrous consequences, so take your time when ordering and installing a hitch.

Hitches are categorized by different ratings, depending on the Gross Vehicle Weight (GVW). GVW is simply the weight of the trailer plus the weight of the boat plus the weight of all the gear inside the boat.

Type I hitches are for 2,000 pounds GVW or less, which puts them below our needs. Type II hitches can handle up to 3,500 pounds, Type III from 3,500 to 6,000 pounds, and Type IV from 6,000 to 10,000 pounds.

In addition to the GVW for determining the proper hitch, you'll need to consider the so-called "tongue weight," which is the downward force exerted by the trailer on the trailer hitch. Tongue weight is the force that turns so many tow cars into tail-draggers with the rear bumper banging and scraping on every dip in the road.

Type I and II hitches are normally nonequalizing hitches, so the full tongue weight is forcing the rear of the car down. Types III and IV are usually equalizing hitches, with weight-carrying platforms installed under the tow car.

The weight-equalizing hitch is more difficult to explain than it is to use, but it simply transfers a large portion of the tongue weight toward the front of the tow car, allowing it to ride level.

An equalizing hitch removes much of the stress of towing from the rear suspension and distributes it over the entire car. The result is that the trailer hitch simply pulls the trailer rather than supporting it.

You'll still need tongue weight to keep the trailer from whiplashing as you drive along, but the equalizing hitch will distribute it more evenly. For Type II hitches, the tongue weight should be 7 percent to 10 percent of the GVW. For the larger Type III and IV hitches, you shouldn't have more than 300 pounds on the hitch. Don't go too light, however, or the trailer will sway. You may want to redistribute the weight inside the boat to put more load on the tongue if you have a sway problem.

15

Towing

Before taking off for the water with your boat, you'll need to prepare the boat and trailer for the trip. Stow your gear inside the boat carefully, keeping in mind that you don't want to affect the weight balance from front to rear of the trailer. Don't stash all the heavy items up in the bow or you'll overload the tongue. Make sure that all heavy items, or gear with sharp edges, are securely fastened down. Lightweight gear, like sleeping bags and sails, can be left loose or used to hold down other equipment.

If you have to travel any distance, consider leaving the water and fuel tanks empty. You'll reduce the trailer weight by several hundred pounds, which will make towing easier and will improve the gas mileage.

If you have a boat cover, fasten it down securely. A loose, flapping cover can cut your mileage by several miles per gallon, not to mention the possibility of tearing the cover. The cover should be well padded around all sharp edges on your boat, and any snaps or fasteners should be protected from contact with your hull.

Check to see that the tiedown lines are snug, but not too tight because you could bend the boat by exerting too much pressure on them. What you want is for the boat and trailer to move as a single unit, so don't allow any slack in them either.

Protect the wire rigging of your mast while trailering, since the wind can toss it around and kink it or fatigue the swages. The best method is to tie the loose rigging securely to the mast at several points, particularly near swages. The remaining wire should be coiled in large loops and tied to the deck.

Be sure to close all portholes and hatches securely, or you're liable to scoop up a squadron of insects. If you plan to drive more than a short distance, lock the hatches. Unlocked hatches are an invitation to burglars.

Give your trailer a good once-over, no matter how short a distance it is to the launching ramp. When attaching to the tow car, be sure that the hitch is fully seated on the trailer ball and that the latch is securely closed. One way to check is to crank the tongue jack up against the closed hitch. It should start to lift the car if it is securely fastened.

Check to see that the safety chains are attached, using a shackle rather than a simple S hook. The chains should cross under the tongue to provide a cradle for the trailer if it does pull loose from the car. Make sure the emergency brake chain is attached to both the tow car and the brake system.

Have someone check the trailer lights for operation while you actuate the brakes, headlights, and turn signals.

As soon as you start the car rolling, test the brakes to see if they are working properly. Better to find out at 5 mph than at 55 mph on the freeway.

Nobody automatically knows how to handle a trailer until he or she has practiced, so don't feel embarrassed by taking your new boat and trailer out to a big parking lot and trying it out at slow speeds. You'll be much happier if you master towing, and especially backing up, before you get near the launching ramp.

When driving with your new tow, keep in mind that you're at least twice as long as you were before. Allow plenty of room for both stopping and starting, and remember to leave extra space on corners or you'll have the trailer bumping over curbs. Know the height of your boat and trailer with the mast stowed on deck, and keep an eye open for bridges or other obstructions that might hit your boat.

Even a lightweight boat will affect the handling of your car. You'll probably find that it has a tendency to oversteer or go straight instead of turning. This is because of the weight behind the car pushing it ahead. Steer smoothly and see if you have to turn the wheel more than normal to achieve the proper curve to the car/trailer package.

Make allowances for the reduced power of your car when you pull into traffic, and be cautious when you pass someone. The most common mistake is to closely tailgate a slower car while you await a chance to pass, which overlooks your need for extra room to stop if the car ahead should slam on his brakes. Pick passing spots that give plenty of clear road to swing out, pick up speed, and swing your long load back into line.

On multilane highways in most states, cars with trailers must use the far-right lane for cruising, with the second lane for passing only. Check the laws before you get a ticket.

The trickiest part of handling a car/trailer rig is in crosswinds when sudden gusts can set the trailer swaying behind you. While your first reaction is usually to steer drastically while hitting the brakes, both are wrong. Make minor steering corrections and tap the brakes gently to get the rig under control.

If the winds persist and it isn't comfortable to travel at a lower speed, simply pull off the road and wait the winds out. You'll be a lot more relaxed when you reach your destination.

Keep an eye on the rearview mirrors, especially when you're on single-lane roads. If you see a line of cars stuck behind you, pull off and let them pass. It's common courtesy, and you may prevent an accident if one tries to jam past you without sufficient room.

Stop regularly to check the entire rig. The best plan is to stop after the first 10 miles to see if anything is immediately apparent, and every 100 miles after that. You'll probably need to get out and stretch at that distance anyway, and you'll know that everything is secure.

If you have a tandem axle trailer and you experience problems with the rig swaying behind you, experiment with reducing the tire pressure in the front tires. Some rigs track perfectly with the front tires running 5 pounds less pressure than the rears.

Backing up is the nemesis of every trailer driver, and, no matter how much experience you have, it's still something you have to concentrate on. Take your trailer and boat to an empty lot and set up some markers that won't damage the trailer if you back over them. Beer cans or cardboard boxes are perfect.

Your first step in mastering reverse is to learn to back straight.

There's no particular trick to it except that you'll overcompensate with the wheel to start with. Once you find that very little movement of the steering wheel will create very large direction changes in the trailer, you're ready to move on.

Turning is more difficult in reverse. It's a game of opposites, with the wheel turning in an opposite direction to where you want the trailer to go. The best teacher is experience. You'll find that the most common occurrence is the jackknife, where the trailer ends up at right angles to the car and no matter how you turn the wheel, you still can't get it to straighten out. The solution is simple—pull forward to straighten the trailer and then resume your backing turn.

A word of caution here: even experienced drivers find themselves concentrating so intently on the trailer that they forget to watch where their car is going. Most launching-ramp fender-benders occur when the front of the tow car has turned into another car or trailer. So watch what's happening in front of you as well as behind you, particularly when you're turning.

An hour of practice in a parking lot will give you more than enough confidence to venture down to the launching ramp.

Living with the Trailerable Sailboat

16

~·~·~·~·~·~·

Launching
and Retrieving

Launching your trailer boat is a lot simpler than it looks, especially
when you've seen a disorganized crew attempt it. The key to the entire
process is to move slowly and have a specific plan for who does what.

When you first arrive at the launching ramp, don't drive directly to
the ramp area. Park your car at a distance and do all your preliminary
work there so that you won't take up valuable ramp space. If possible,
try to pick the best ramp in the area for your first few launches. Once
you've built up your confidence, you can start using dirt ramps or
beaches. But for now you should find a concrete or asphalt ramp with
a pier next to it for final rigging.

Walk down to the water's edge and study the situation. Take into
account the depth of the water, the size of the ramp, and the direction
of the wind. Life will be easier if the wind is pushing you *off* the ramp
rather than back on it, and a nearby pier will let you rig the sails without
hurrying. Don't hesitate to ask questions—fools are the ones who rush
in.

Once you're satisfied that this is a good ramp, get the boat ready for launching. You'll want to remove the cover and store it in the car, sort out the various rigging, and step the mast.

Every boat has its own idiosyncracies concerning the mast and what the easiest method is to raise it. Talk to other owners, and see how they've simplified the process. You can probably use the boom and mainsheet to add to your power if the mast tips forward or a short strut if the mast tips aft.

Once you have the mast up, finish by attaching all the remaining rigging and hook up the boom. It's much easier to handle all these details now rather than waiting until after the launching, because you'll have loose gear all over the deck at a time when you want to move around easily. If you'll need the outboard, start it before you're at the ramp. You can let it run for a few moments without damage, and you'll know that it will restart easily in the water.

When you have the boat ready, remove or disconnect the trailer lights and allow them to cool. If both the lights and the wheel bearings have cooled before you submerge them, you won't damage them with cold water.

Before you move the trailer, look around for overhead obstructions such as power lines or lights that might catch your mast. Have a spotter walk beside the boat as you back slowly toward the ramp. You should have outlined your plans to the crew so that each person knows what is expected of him or her. Prearrange some hand signals so that your spotter won't have to shout at you to stop, turn, or indicate distance. Your spotter should have a line attached to the bow of the boat and one to the stern as well to control the boat once it floats off the trailer.

When you've reached the point where the boat will float off, stop the car, put the transmission in park, set the hand brake, and chock the rear tires so you won't have to worry about the car.

You may have to climb up on the trailer and give the boat a shove or rock it from side to side to break it free from the trailer. Once the boat is free, leave it for your crew to handle, and immediately move the car to a parking area so that you won't hold up other boats waiting to launch. A simple trick is to make your tire chocks out of large chunks of wood with a line attached to each one. Tie the line to the bumper and you'll be able to drive up the ramp without having to retrieve the chocks which will trail along obediently behind the car.

Once the boat is at the dock, you can set about preparing to sail or power away. Don't be in a hurry, and make sure everything is stowed, fastened, tied, or secured before you depart. A checklist, like the ones that pilots use before landing or takeoff, is a good idea to make for this stage. That way you won't forget to hook up the backstay or tighten a turnbuckle.

Retrieving the boat is essentially the reverse of the above operation. You'll sail or power into the dock at the ramp, and derig the boat to where it is ready to be put on the trailer.

Bring the car and trailer to the ramp, and back them straight down to the water. It's often hard to see the trailer, particularly on steep ramps, and a pair of removable bamboo poles at each corner can make backing easier as well as give your crew something to line up on as they head for the trailer.

Secure the car as you did before, and have the boat brought over to the trailer. You'll need to know how deep the trailer must be submerged for easy loading, and tape markers at various points on the trailer can assure you that you're deep enough.

Attach the winch line to the bow fitting of your boat, and line the boat up on the rollers. This is the most difficult part, particularly when a cross wind is blowing the boat sideways. If you take a little strain on the winch line when the bow is on the first roller, you can use the rudder to scull the boat into line without worrying about keeping the bow in place.

Once lined up, have your crew move aft and start up your winch to pull the boat onto the trailer. If you have large carpeted pads, splash water on them first or squirt liquid detergent over them to make them slippery. Stand away from the winch and wire for safety, and continue to pull the boat onto the trailer. If it stops suddenly or hangs up on something, stop the winch to keep it from stalling or breaking the wire.

Once the boat is securely in place on the trailer, have the crew climb off the boat. You can now drive to a parking place for final disassembly before you head for home.

Don't forget to check all the items you checked before leaving home, both on the trailer and on the boat. If there is a hose available, rinse off boat, trailer, bearings and brakes so that you'll have an easier task when you get home.

17

~~~~~~

Boat Handling

Probably the first bit of seamanship that you'll have to perform on your new boat is docking. If you've launched off the trailer, you'll move the boat to a pier for the final preparations. In calm water and light breezes, you should have no problem as you get used to your boat. If there seems to be a lot of wind, you'd be wise to postpone your first cruise until the next day.

What you'll need to learn, as quickly as possible, is what to expect from your boat in various situations. For example, when you stop the engine or luff the sails, how far will the boat coast and under how much control? You'll find that at the very end of its inertia, when speed is at a minimum, you won't have good control and you'll have to really move the tiller to affect the boat's course.

In most situations such as anchoring, picking up a mooring buoy, or docking, knowing what to expect from your boat will make life much more relaxed. To that end, you can spend a useful afternoon by picking out a small buoy in protected water and seeing how close to it you can make the boat stop. Armed with that experience, you'll be ready for most situations. Just keep in mind that wind and wave will affect your trailerable sailboat more than it will affect most other vessels because you're lighter and shallower. If the sea is choppy, each wave will act as a drag brake when you go through it. At the same time, the wind will tend to push your boat easily. So take the breeze into consideration as you plan your approaches.

Let's look at powering first. Your eventual goal is to have the boat lying alongside the dock since climbing off via the bow is awkward. Approach the dock at an angle and be prepared to slow and shift your engine. If the engine isn't convenient to the tiller, the helmsman should probably station one of the crew at the engine to control it. As you near the dock, simply put the engine in neutral and turn the boat so that you parallel the dock. When you reach the spot you want, reverse the engine and have the crew step off with the dock lines.

Docking under sail is trickier because you don't have reverse and because you're more dependent on the wind direction. Until you gain confidence in yourself and the boat, postpone docking under sail.

The easiest docks to use when sailing have the wind blowing either directly off or at least parallel to them. If the wind is paralleling the dock, your approach is similar to the one under power. Sail toward the dock at an angle, easing out your sails to slow down as you near it. Turn *into* the wind and coast along next to the dock until you have almost stopped. At that point, use the dock lines to tie up and then drop your sails.

If the wind is blowing off the dock, you'll probably find it easier to sail parallel to the dock and then head directly toward your chosen spot with the sails luffing. If you've gauged your coasting ability right, you'll stop and someone can step off with a bow line. Once you've lowered your sails, you can turn the boat alongside the dock. If you find yourself approaching too fast, you can "backwind" the mainsail by pushing it out like a brake against the wind to slow the boat. If you don't have enough momentum to reach the dock, a little rapid sculling back and forth with the rudder will probably push you the remaining distance. If not, simply try again.

The toughest dock to use under sail is one toward which the wind is blowing. In this situation, you'd do well to drop your sails, or at least your mainsail, and then approach the dock as though you are under power with the wind as your engine. Your jib can be luffed as you near the dock, since it can flap directly in front of the boat. The mainsail can't be let out far enough to luff before the boom hits the rigging, so never try to approach a downwind dock with the mainsail up. It's like parking a car with the throttle to the floor.

Grief can be avoided by explaining your plans to the crew. The fenders should be hung over the side nearest the dock, the bow and stern lines should be ready for use, and your crew should be prepared to help fend off the boat and stop it. Emphasize that crew members shouldn't step ashore until you tell them to because many eager crews underestimate the jumping distance and end up in the drink. Besides, in a light boat like a trailerable sailboat, the force of one person leaping off the bow is enough to alter your course and perhaps foul up your approach. The bow line should be secured first, followed by the stern line and then any other lines to keep the boat from bouncing around.

Picking up a mooring is much like docking, except that it's usually easier because you have a clear area around it and don't have to worry about hitting other boats or a dock. Station someone forward with a boat hook to catch the buoy, and then approach from downwind with your sails luffing. With too little momentum, you won't reach the buoy. Too much and you'll zip past. Warn your crew not to try and stop the boat if you're going too fast—the mooring is liable to pull someone right off the boat as you pass.

In spite of what many experienced sailors will try to tell you, anchoring is no black art. There is really no mystery to it, regardless of how they clutter up the nautical vocabulary with words like *scope, rode, flukes,* and the like. You are simply attaching the boat to the bottom of the ocean with a piece of nylon—nothing more, nothing less. Probably the most distressing thing about anchoring is that, in most coves, you'll have spectators aboard surrounding boats watching you. It's a favorite activity—seeing how well (or how badly) someone anchors. Don't be dismayed by these eyes. Just plan your actions ahead of time.

First, you need to pick a spot. You'll want to be protected from wind and current, and you'll want to be in water deep enough so that you don't go aground at low tide. If you have a choice, you'll want to be over a type of bottom that makes for easy anchoring, such as sand rather than weeds. With a trailerable sailboat, you can often moor much closer to shore than bigger and deeper yachts, so don't be afraid to find your own niche. Just ask yourself: "Why isn't anyone else here?"

Be sure that your anchor is rigged and ready to go before you start your approach. A tangled anchor is what all those beady eyes are hoping for. The easiest way to store an anchor aboard a trailerable, if

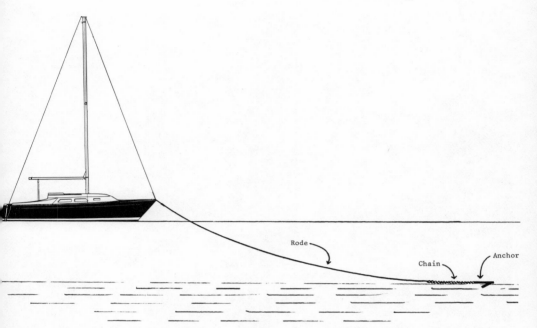

A simplified drawing of a trailerable sailboat at anchor. The length of the rode should be at least five times the depth of the water, preferably seven or eight times the depth for security. The chain helps the anchor "bite" into the bottom as well as absorb shocks.

you don't have an anchor well, is in a plastic laundry tub that you simply carry on deck. The line is coiled inside ready for use, yet you can store it under the cockpit out of the way.

When you've gained some experience, you can sail in and anchor, just to impress all the spectators. For now, use the engine for security. You should have your sails down and either neatly furled or stowed away. You need the deck area up forward, and you don't want the crew falling over stray lines.

Take a look to see how everyone else is anchored. If they are using only a single bow anchor, then you should also. If they are using bow and stern anchors, plan for that. If they have only single anchors, make sure that you've left enough room in your planned spot so that you'll be free to swing as the wind shifts without hitting other boats.

An anchor bucket with anchor, chain, and rode ready for use. The bucket can be stored under the cockpit seats, and the vented sides allow the line to dry.

Your chart will indicate the depth of water where you plan to anchor as well as the bottom type, but you might want to check with your depth sounder as a precaution.

Scope is a fancy word for the ratio of anchor line to water depth. For example, if you anchor in 20 feet of water and you let out 100 feet of anchor line, your scope is 5 to 1 (5:1). Scope is measured from the deck attachment of your boat, but trailerable boats are low enough that you can simply figure water depth alone. A scope of 5:1 is considered minimum for most conditions, and you're better with 7:1 or 8:1. In heavy winds or storms, the more scope you have, the better, since it allows your anchor to bite more efficiently into the bottom.

How do you know how much scope you have? You should mark your anchor line, and the easiest way is to buy numbered tags at a marine store and place them every 20 feet on your line.

Approach your planned anchor location under power and heading into the wind, if possible. Continue past your spot to a distance upwind equal to your planned scope. Using reverse, stop the boat and have your crew let the anchor overboard at this point.

You should have some hand signals, because it's often hard to hear over an outboard and spectators always enjoy husbands yelling at angry wives. Don't toss the anchor overboard—that's considered bad style and could tangle the anchor. Let it gently into the water until you feel it hit bottom. At that point, either back the boat up using reverse or let the wind carry you back until you've reached the proper scope. Give the anchor rode a sharp tug to help set the anchor, and then sit back. Take a look around to see where you are in relation to other boats or landmarks, and then wait to see if the anchor is firmly set. If you find yourself drifting backward, then you're dragging the anchor. More scope is the usual solution, and you should let it out with frequent tugs rather than just throwing more line over the side. Another sharp tug at the end and you'll probably be set for the night.

If you need to set two anchors, follow the procedure for the single anchor, but let the boat drift backward until you are over the place where you want to set your stern anchor. Let it down, and then either pull or power your boat back into the middle between the two anchors. If you're very confident of your abilities, you can drop the stern anchor first, and then power up to the bow-anchor spot, but your problems can be multiplied if the bow anchor doesn't hold immediately.

The method of sailing in to anchor is the same, except that you have to be quicker. With enough speed to reach your bow-anchor spot, head the boat into the wind and let the sails luff. When the boat has almost stopped moving, hopefully at the place you want the bow anchor, let it over the side. At that point, you can let the boat drift back. Once you're sure the anchor is set, you can drop your sails and set the stern anchor. If you drop your sails too early, you may find yourself rushing to get sails and anchor up while you fend off other boats when the anchor drags.

To hoist, or weigh, anchor, simply reverse the steps. Drop back to pick up the stern anchor, if you have one, then power up to a point where the anchor line is straight up and down. Stop the boat, and let the crew pull the anchor up and coil the line in the basket or locker.

If the anchor won't break loose from the bottom, the easiest method in a trailerable sailboat is to move several crewmembers to the bow (forcing it down) and then cleat the anchor line off sungly. Move the same crew to the stern, and the resulting buoyancy will usually lever the anchor free.

If you have a chance, practice anchoring before you have to perform in front of an audience. Remember not to yell regardless of how dumb your crew may seem.

18

˜˙˜˙˜˙˜·

Seamanship

Seamanship is a loose term covering all aspects of handling a boat safely, and the general concepts apply to trailerable sailboats as well as to other yachts.

For everyday situations, you'll probably find little to test your boat-handling skills other than docking or anchoring. Practice will soon perfect those skills. But there are other areas that simply can't be practiced, such as sailing in storm conditions, and you'll have to rely on outside advice to prepare yourself.

Few trailerable sailboats cross oceans, but you can find yourself caught in an afternoon squall that can seem every bit as nasty as a North Atlantic gale. If you've paid attention to the weather reports and have kept an eye open, you shouldn't be too surprised by an afternoon sneaker, but you may be too far from port to get back before it hits.

In that situation, the trailerable sailboat will react differently than the conventional keel sailboat. The first element that you'll have to deal with is wind, and it can build up rapidly. For that reason, you should have jiffy reefing on your mainsail so that you can reduce the area quickly. Because of the narrow width of your swing keel, trailerable sailboats are more sensitive to balance between main and jib than a full-keeled sailboat, so you can't simply drop the mainsail and expect to keep full control. In instances where you have plenty of distance from shore and you expect the squall to be a short one, simply dropping your

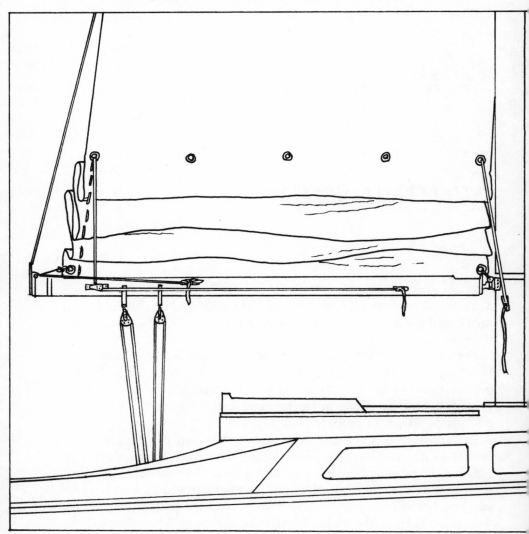

This drawing shows the basic "jiffy-reefing" system used by most trailerable sailboats. When the mainsail needs to be reefed, the halyard is released to lower the sail. At the same time, the two reefing lines that lead through the forward and aft reef point grommets are pulled tight. The result is that the sail is reduced in area to the line of grommets and further lines can be tied through each reef point to equalize the strain on the entire sail.

sails and retiring to the dry cabin may be the best plan. But if you need to keep going, you'll have to reduce sail by increments. If, for example, you have a genoa and mainsail up as the wind increases, you'll probably want to switch to your smaller working jib first. This counters advice for bigger boats, where a reefed main is recommended first. You'll sail just as well with your smaller jib, and, since you have a small and unstable foredeck, it will be easier to make the jib change before the wind is blowing full force. Bigger boats with bigger crews and bigger foredecks can wait to change headsails. Do yours first.

As the wind continues to increase, you'll want to tuck the jiffy reef into the mainsail. At this point, most trailerable sailboats are fresh out of sail-reduction methods. You probably don't have another set of reef points for the mainsail, nor do you have a smaller jib available. Happily, you'll probably have a manageable boat with this shortened sail, and you can ride out the squall.

One trick to keep in mind is the so-called "fisherman's reef," which was developed by old salts who had no way of reefing their sails. They simply allowed a large luff to form in the mainsail, which effectively reduced the sail area. Don't allow the mainsail to flog completely unless you're really out of control, because you'll start breaking the battens and you may tear a seam. But you can sail for a long time with only the batten area of the mainsail filled and the rest of the sail luffing.

Because a trailerable sailboat is light, it will react to puffs more rapidly than other sailboats. Therefore, keep a hand on the mainsheet at all times so that you can ease it quickly in a gust. You'll find that, if you have sailing room to head any direction, you'll be most comfortable on a close reach. Running is dangerous if the wind is shifting at all (which could cause a jibe) and beating is a lot of work and not much fun in a squall.

After the wind, you're liable to have big seas, although this only applies in the ocean or in large lakes. Surprisingly, the seas can build up rapidly when there is sufficient wind, and you may find yourself pounding into huge swells. The trick to sailing comfortably and effectively in big swells is all in the steering.

Don't try to steer a straight course. A steady zigzag will get you over the crests and through the troughs with much less fuss. As you start down into the trough, head slightly away from the wind, and when you

This small sailboat is going to have to prepare for some bad weather as a black squall can be seen on the horizon. A small jib and jiffy reefing will usually be enough to handle the squall.

go up the crest, head slightly upwind. By following this S course, you're preventing the bow from dropping suddenly into the trough and from getting caught broadside on the crest.

Because trailerables are light and don't have much inertia, don't try to punch through waves. They'll stop you dead, the bow will slide sideways, and the next gust will knock you over. Try to steer over and around the steepest swells and keep the boat moving at all times, even if you have to ease your sails and reach off slightly. If you try to bull through the waves, you'll have wet, slow, and uncomfortable sailing.

If the wind and sea continue or increase to the point where you are concerned about the safety of the boat, it is time to heave-to.

There are several ways of doing this in a trailerable sailboat; pick the one that fits your own needs at the time. The most common method is to tack without releasing the jib, so that the sail is backwinded across the upwind side of the foredeck against the shrouds. Ease the main and hold or lash the tiller to the leeward side. What you've accomplished is a balance, and the boat will drift sideways slowly with a zigzag course like a falling leaf.

The wind pressure on the jib will force the bow down until the mainsail starts to fill, and the rudder to leeward then forces the bow back up. Don't kid yourself, in a lot of wind and sea this won't be very comfortable, but it is safe.

A second method available to trailerables is to drop sail and let the wind push you downwind, assuming you have plenty of room. A light boat like this can actually start surfing in front of the waves, and the ride will be fairly calm. You should become concerned when the waves grow very large and you don't have good control as you surf down the faces. This can lead to a broach, where the boat is suddenly thrown sideways and tends to be knocked down.

When you're experiencing this condition, drag something astern to slow the boat and increase your control. The easiest thing to drag is your anchor line, which should be strung out from each stern cleat in a long loop. The drag from the line is usually enough to slow your headway to a reasonable pace.

At the other end of the spectrum, you may find yourself nearly becalmed without an engine. Light boats like trailerables do well in these conditions, if you have the knowledge and patience to make them go.

Your first order is to keep everyone still. Nothing slows a boat as

At the other end of the wind spectrum from a squall is a calm. You should be prepared to deal with light winds as well as gales.

much as someone jumping up and stomping below for a cold beer. If you have to move, move gently.

Have the crew sit to leeward and forward of the cockpit along the rail. This accomplishes two things: it gets the stern out of the water, which will cut your drag, and it heels the boat to leeward, which will help fill the sails. If the day is hot and the crew doesn't want to sit on the side decks, they can sit below on the lee side settee and accomplish the same result.

You should have yarn telltales on your shrouds, and you might take up smoking at this moment so that you can see where the smoke drifts. Once you've determined where the wind is, however light, set your sails accordingly. Loosen all the adjustments on your sails: outhaul, downhaul, and jib halyard, to release the tension. You'll want baggy sails in light air. Be careful that you don't "overtrim" the sails either, by sheeting them in too tight.

Once you have the sails set and the wind direction established, you'll have to steer the boat very gently. Keep an eye on the telltales, watch for wind indications on the water ahead, and keep the boat moving even if it isn't exactly on the course you want. Once you build up a little headway, you can probably keep it.

On another subject of seamanship, you may find yourself needing a tow or offering one. Before you do either, you should be prepared.

Passing the tow line may be difficult to do in this situation, especially if there is a big sea. If you can't toss the line to the other boat, try floating it over on a life preserver. The tow line itself should be the heaviest line you have aboard, which is often your anchor line.

If you're doing the towing, don't fasten the line to the stern cleats because the stern must turn freely to steer the boat. On trailerable sailboats, the winches are usually the strongest attachment point, and you should put a few turns around one winch and then secure the line. Make sure that the tow line doesn't hit anything in the cockpit, because it can bend or break pulpits and stanchions.

If you're being towed, your bow cleat may or may not be sturdy enough to stand the loads. You should run the line back around the base of your mast, which is well supported.

The length of the tow line will depend on where you are: in a harbor, keep it short for maneuverability; in open water, give yourself plenty of distance so that shocks are absorbed by the line, not by your cleats.

19

~~~~~~

Emergencies

Murphy's Law was probably devised with the sailor in mind: anything that can happen, will. Emergencies aboard a trailerable sailboat tend to revolve around one of two elements: the people or the boat. They interrelate, of course, and damage to the boat can sometimes end in personal injury. Accidents happen at the worst times, and your best prevention is simply to be prepared in your mind and in equipment for anything that might happen.

The number-one rule in any crisis situation is to account for your crew. Before taking *any* other action to solve the problem, make sure that everyone is aboard and in good condition. The skipper should assert his authority, even though he may never use it at other times, so that all decisions and commands are made by one person. When everyone decides to work independently, confusion is the result.

Once you've checked the crew, your own ingenuity will determine the outcome of the crisis. Stay calm, assess the extent of the problem, and your attitude will be passed on to the crew.

Every type of emergency has its own priorities. You'll need to consider each possibility in the light of your boat, your experience, and the equipment you have on board.

COLLISION. There are two types of collision: with another vessel and with a solid object of some kind. Most boat-to-boat collisions are caused by someone not watching where he or she is going; these seldom result in severe damage to the hull. Aboard a trailerable sailboat, your gravest danger in a collision with another boat is that the other vessel may break some of your rigging and dismast you or cause injuries aboard your own boat. It is collision with other solid objects that are below the water line, such as rocks, logs, or pilings, that can hole your boat and sink it.

If you're holed below the water line and water is pouring in, your first task (after getting everyone into life jackets) is to find and stop the leak. While you're doing that, someone else should man the bilge pump or start using a large bucket to keep the water down.

Once you've found the hole, you can usually stuff it with pillows, blankets, sleeping bags, or other materials that will slow the water flow. If you are far from shore or haul-out facilities, you should wedge the stuffing in place using a boat hook, a cabinet door, or anything else at hand. A collision mat for the outside can be jury-rigged out of an awning or a sail. The collision mat covers the damaged area and is positioned by lines under the hull as well as fore and aft. Water pressure will force the mat against the hole and further slow the flow.

At this point, you'll have to decide whether your own pumps can stay ahead of the flow or whether you need to radio for Coast Guard assistance. If you're near shore, the Coast Guard will probably send a small cutter to aid you; if you're quite a distance out, they will air-drop a gas-powered bilge pump.

FIRE. Surrounded by water, fire is one of the most frightening disasters afloat because there is no place to run. Aboard trailerable sailboats, the problems of fire are minimal and the stove is the primary culprit. With an alcohol stove, a saucepan of water sloshed on the burning area will probably put the fire out by diluting the alcohol enough so that it won't burn. Be sure that you've got it all, though, because an alcohol fire is hard to see.

If you still have fire on your hands, it's time to grab a fire extinguisher. Most boats carry dry chemical extinguishers, and these are always sprayed at the base of the flame with a sweeping motion.

WATER ENTRY. This is separate from collision because you're likely to find out about this when someone says, "Hey, dad, the floor's under water!" There aren't too many places that water can enter a trailerable sailboat, but your first task is still to find out where the leak is. Start with obvious possibilities such as the through-hull fittings for the sink or cockpit drains, or the centerboard pivot bolthole. Most likely, the problem is something as simple as a broken hose on a through-hull fitting or a hose clamp that has slipped off. If that is the case, repair is fairly simple. A supply of corks comes in useful in a situation like this, since one will either fit the hole or can be carved to size.

If you have trouble locating the leak but it appears to be near the water line, you can often raise the trouble area out of the water by tacking and having your crew sit to leeward to heel the boat more than normal. Once you've located the leak, you can handle it as in a collision. MAN OVERBOARD. With a trailerable sailboat, this is less of a crisis than it is with a big ocean racer charging along at top speed. Because a small boat is more maneuverable, you can spin around rapidly and retrieve your errant crew member.

Nevertheless, there are some basic precautions and procedures that your crew should understand and practice. First, throw a life preserver to the person in the water. Second, one of your crew should be detailed to do nothing except watch the person in the water, especially when there is a chop or even small swells, since a head is a very small object in a big ocean. Don't let the person watching do anything else!

Your fastest return path is to jibe the boat immediately and then luff up into the wind next to the person in the water. At this point, you'll have to haul a sodden and tired person aboard, which is easier said than done. You should have a boarding ladder or a line with rope loops for just such situations as well as for when you swim from your boat. DISMASTING. This isn't too rare among trailerable sailboats because crews forget to tighten rigging or the wire is kinked during the raising of the spar and it eventually fails. Your first intimation of disaster is when the entire mast falls into the water next to you. Since almost all trailerable sailboats have deck-stepped masts, it has probably either broken the hinge or torn the step off the deck. In either case, you're faced with a tangle of aluminum mast, wire and rope rigging, and dacron sails.

After checking your crew, you'll want to get the cumbersome mast under control so that you don't roll into it and puncture your hull. Masts of this size aren't so heavy that you can't simply manhandle it onto the deck. Once there, you can start to pull in the tangle of rigging. Don't ever start your engine until you're absolutely sure that the water is free of lines and rigging. Otherwise you'll wrap one around the prop, and then you'll have no way of getting home.

Lash the mast in place, and set some of the crew to straightening things up by removing the jib (usually easy) and the mainsail (usually difficult). Don't risk tearing the sails, and tie them to prevent flapping if you can't get them off the mast.

BROKEN RIGGING. You may be able to prevent a dismasting if you notice that a crucial strand of rigging has broken. For example, if the headstay breaks, the mast is supported by the jib but will soon give way. Turning immediately downwind so that the strain is released from the headstay will save the mast, and you can jury-rig a headstay and then power home with everything intact. If the backstay breaks, you can turn into the wind to achieve the same thing. If one of your shrouds or a spreader fails, an immediate tack will ease the dangerous load on the mast.

If you carry small lengths of spare line, you'll be able to jury-rig replacements for your rigging so that you can get home.

BROKEN RUDDER. This is usually caused by hitting an underwater obstruction and either breaking the rudder or tearing it loose from the stern. In either case, you'll have to get your sails down as quickly as possible to regain control. If you have an outboard, you can probably use it to steer home by turning it rather than the rudder. If you don't have an outboard, you'll have to produce a makeshift rudder out of a spinnaker pole, a paddle, or a boat hook. Don't try to carry full sail with the replacement rudder; it won't stand much load. You're better off using only the jib (which can easily be luffed) and gently heading home.

PERSONAL INJURY. The most common injuries around trailerable sailboats are cuts and burns; your first-aid kit can deal with these easily. More severe injuries, such as broken bones or the occasional concussion from standing tall under a low boom, should be considered medical emergencies and handled as such. If you have VHF or CB, use the radio to call for assistance. The Coast Guard or the local Harbor Patrol will probably set up an ambulance to meet you at the nearest dock or, if you're offshore, will send a fast boat if you can transfer the injured person.

If you're far offshore with a severely injured person, you'll need a helicopter evacuation. It's not easy aboard a small sailboat, but it can be done. If you have a dinghy, put the injured person in it with someone to assist, and the chopper will lift that person from the small boat, which is away from your mast and rigging. Prepare a written description of the accident and pin it to the injured person to aid the doctor aboard the helicopter.

Don't ever rely solely on the marine first-aid kits that are sold in stores and sporting-goods shops. They are rarely more than first-aid cream and bandages. Start with a waterproof box, and add all the equipment you think you might ever need. Basic kits don't have enough space to personalize them to fit your own needs. A list of useful medical supplies for the trailerable sailboat is in the Appendix and should be assembled with the help and advice of your family doctor.

20

Storage

Getting it all in is the problem. If you survey the amount of food, provisions, and boat gear that has to be fitted into your trailerable sailboat, you might throw your hands up in dismay. It can be done, and fairly easily, if you approach it methodically. Let's start with the basics and see what can be done with this mountain of equipment.

Sails don't have to be stowed belowdecks, although that's where they should be for security when trailering or leaving the boat for any length of time. The mainsail can furl on the boom; that gets rid of one problem. Unless you want to be tidy or leave your boat afloat, you won't need to cover the main. The jibs or genoas can be bagged neatly and left on deck after the day's sail. One good method of handling them is to leave them hanked to the headstay, to bag them from the aft end including sheets, and then to hoist the bag off the deck with the halyard. This gives you free access to the bow cleats for anchoring or docking and helps the sail dry quickly.

When you're under way, the extra sails will probably reside best on the forward bunks. You won't need that sleeping area, so spinnakers and extra jibs can be tossed out of the way until you're ready to settle in for the night, when they can be moved on deck.

Except for the anchor well, the best solution to anchor gear is the plastic laundry tub mentioned earlier. It can be kept out of the way under a cockpit hatch until needed.

Make some decisions about individual items. You'll want to keep certain equipment, like flashlights and binoculars, readily accessible. For the remainder of your gear, ask yourself how often it will be needed. Depending on the answer, you'll know where you have to stow that equipment.

Try to keep similar items together. For example, instead of putting the screwdriver in one drawer, the pliers in another, and the hammer under the seat, find or make a place to keep the tools together. Last, determine which items are fragile or subject to damage. You won't want to put paper napkins in the lockers under the seats because that's a damp area. It's perfect, though, for canned goods.

Take inventory of your boat and see where you already have storage. In most trailerable sailboats, you'll find some drawers and shelves around the galley, bins under the bunks, and a large area under the cockpit that are empty.

Starting with the bunk bins, you'll probably guess that they can hold a great many items. They will, which you'll learn when the item you need is on the bottom. The key to stowing equipment is to make it available without major disruptions. Look for plastic bins such as dishpans or plastic shoe or sweater boxes that will fit into these areas. You can use them to subdivide the bins into compartments that lift out easily when you're searching for something. They'll also protect the stored goods from dampness that is caused when the hull sweats condensation.

Your clothing and essentials are handled best by duffel bags. Every crew member should have one. They're available in marine stores or can be made at home. A duffel bag should have a large zippered opening so that you don't have to grope around for a pair of socks, and some duffels have areas lined with waterproofed material that can hold damp swim suits or dirty clothes without affecting the other clothing. The duffels can sit on each bunk during the day, or they can be tossed up forward out of the way. Some duffels have provisions so that they can be snapped to the bulkhead above each bunk, which solves the storage problem.

Give the galley the same cold appraisal and decide how best to use the storage that is already provided. Unfortunately, drawers are great space-wasters. You'd probably be better off with bins, and some owners have performed such conversions. They put their utensils into one plastic bin, cutlery into another, dry goods in another, and just lift out what they need.

Don't give up if you haven't enough space. You haven't even started yet. Several companies in various parts of the country produce ready-to-install racks, drawers, cabinets, and more. Everything you need to increase your space is ready to screw into place in either teak or mahogany. If you're handy with tools, you can produce the same items in your own garage.

Look under the cockpit. You'll probably find a cavernous area with lots of empty air. Decide what you can store in there, such as your outboard, the gas tank, sails, and anchor basket, and partition it off to hold each item in place. The partitions can simply be marine plywood fiberglassed into place and then painted white to match the hull. Or you can rely on bigger bins, like laundry tubs, to hold items like life jackets.

If you have steps leading into the cabin, there's probably some space under them for pull-out drawers or bins. You'll want to add a shelf near the hatch so that necessities such as suntan cream, matches, and binoculars will be close at hand.

Pillows are awkward to stow unless you make a pillow cover that converts two pillows into a rectangular cushion that is comfortable for afternoon lazing while protecting the pillows from dirt and damp. A canvas shoe storage bag with multiple pouches can hide small items (even shoes) in a hanging locker while saving space elsewhere. Most marine stores offer miniature hammocks that can be strung behind bunks or in the forward area to hold jackets and sweaters while still allowing full air movement around them.

When stowing food in the galley, glass containers should be avoided at all cost. They can be broken by other objects falling on them, and a cracked jar is just waiting for a hand to cut. Plastic containers are much safer, especially if they can nest inside each other until needed for another use.

Don't hesitate to put shelves or partitions in your icebox to make it more useful. If possible, make the shelves or dividers of clear plastic so that you can see what is below each shelf.

Obviously, the key to any storage system lies in putting things back when you're done with them. It keeps each item protected, and it keeps the small cabin of a trailerable sailboat from becoming claustrophobic.

The boat-show display of one company's offerings of ready-to-install racks, drawers, and other space expanders that are needed in the trailerable sailboat.

21

~~~~~~~

Navigation

Few trailerable sailboat builders make any attempt to set space aside for the navigator on the assumption that there probably won't be much serious navigation done aboard boats of this size. In most cases, that's true, but you're still going to need the basics whenever you venture outside the harbor because you never know when the fog will roll in.

Your basic navigational tool is the nautical chart, and you'll need a place to spread it out. Since the charts are huge by comparison to the space available in your boat, try to find Small Craft charts of the area that you need. These are neatly folded and compacted to a smaller size that fits trailerable sailboats.

Other solutions to the problem of where and how to spread out charts include some commercial products. One such item is a chart roller that unrolls your chart like a scroll while presenting you with a flat working area.

Many parts of the country are now covered by "chart books," which are compilations of the local charts bound into flexible books of a convenient size. They are produced from the government charts and are just as accurate, but more reasonably sized.

If you want to carry charts into the cockpit for further study in rain or spray, chart envelopes are available from marine stores. These are

Most waterways, including lakes and rivers, can develop sudden fogs. The wise sailor has basic navigation gear aboard on all trips and knows how to use it.

clear envelopes with waterproof zippers so that you can read the chart (and mark on it with wax pencil) without damaging the chart.

Probably the most common solution for trailerable-sailboat navigators who crave space to spread out their equipment is to build their own portable chart table. Using light marine plywood, they can produce a folding table held together with a long piano hinge that will suit their own size needs. This chart table can rest on a bunk, on knees in the cockpit, or atop the galley area, if there is space. When not in use, it folds in half and stores under the cockpit seats or under a bunk cushion.

In addition to the local charts, you'll need some simple navigational tools to round out your Magellan outfit. A set of parallel rules for plotting courses and a set of dividers for measuring distances can make your chores easier.

You should already have a good compass mounted securely that has been corrected by a professional compass repair service to eliminate deviation from the metal aboard your boat. The service will supply you with a deviation card so that you'll know the exact accuracy of your compass, but it probably won't be used in most of your navigation.

A trustworthy watch will complete your kit, although it need not be a fancy chronometer. You'll only be timing yourself for short periods of time, so absolute accuracy over spans of five or six hours isn't critical.

You'll need a navigational bookshelf, too, if you plan to do any venturing outside the harbor. A set of tide tables will tell you the highs and lows as well as the times of sunrise and sunset. Many hardware stores give these away as promotional items, or you can buy the big government text.

In addition to your chart, you'll need a copy of the Light List, which will help you to identify all the navigational aids and radio beacons in your area. Last, browse through some of the local boating handbooks or almanacs that are published privately. They contain a wealth of useful information on the boating facilities such as fuel docks, launch ramps, and favorite coves and anchorages.

A basic navigation kit consists of parallel rules, a divider, charts, pencil, watch, and a local cruising guide or almanac. Add to this tide tables, a Light List, and electronic navigation instruments, and you're set.

22

~·~·~·~·~·

Cruising

There's no real difference between an afternoon outing and a vacation cruise aboard your trailerable, except that you'll want to carry more food on your trailerable and you may want to add some equipment to make your boat more comfortable for long periods of time.

One of the keys to comfortable cruising is to have plenty of ventilation below, because you'll be spending half your day inside the cabin sleeping and eating. Don't assume that good ventilation is only for warm climates. A closed-up cabin on a cold day can get pretty ripe with three people below, especially if you're cooking.

Cowl ventilators, mounted on deck, are a good source of fresh air. If possible, have two (one forward and one aft) so that you can use one to suck in air and the other to extract it. Several vents are available with water traps so that they can be used in rain or while sailing.

In warm weather, you might consider adding a wind scoop to your forward hatch when you're sitting at anchor. It is available in marine stores, or you can make one at home easily to fit your hatch. It is simply a big cloth funnel, suspended from your mast or forestay, that forces air down the hatch. You can create quite a gale with a wind scoop.

There aren't many cruising areas without insects of some kind, so be prepared with screens for your portholes and your hatch. Mosquito netting can be fitted with Velcro strips around your forward hatch and main hatch, and most opening ports are supplied with snap-in screens. Don't forget to screen your cowl ventilators, and a small piece of netting taped over the scoop will keep the bugs out.

An awning over the cockpit can make life pleasant in warm weather, and it can make the cockpit seats useful for sleeping in areas where there is a heavy dew. You can produce it yourself out of light nylon, using bamboo poles to hold it out at the edges. Don't make the awning too small, though. It should extend forward of the main hatch and wider than the beam by several inches to grab as much shade as possible.

A dinghy is essential in some areas and simply a convenience in others. If you plan to tie up to piers every night on your cruise, then you don't need a dink. If you plan to anchor, a dinghy is a way of getting ashore as well as providing a diversion for the kids. There are two types of dinghies to consider: hard and soft. The hard dinghy is the traditional wood or fiberglass rowboat. There are some good 6-footers that can carry two people, store on the foredeck upside down, tow well behind the trailerable, and have sailing rigs added for afternoons around the anchorage. Ask for a demonstration before you buy, and use the dinghy as you will when cruising. See how many people it can carry. If it doesn't come close to your normal cruising capacity, you'll be stuck rowing back and forth to ferry people ashore. Be sure that it has a rub rail of canvas or rubber around the gunwale to protect your hull when tied alongside.

Inflatable dinghies are a good solution to the trailerable-sailboat storage problem, although they are more expensive than a hard dink. Inflatables will have to be pumped up before each use, although you can tow them from the stern during a cruise. You'll have to be more careful about dragging them over rocks and shells, although punctures are easily patched. Be sure that the inflatable can carry your crew, and it should have provisions for adding an outboard motor as well.

Seasickness can sometimes be a problem on long cruises, particularly when people get tired. The best solution to the problem is to stay on deck and find a task that requires concentration but little physical strength. Steering is an ideal project. You may also find that a slight change of course will alleviate the motion that brought on the illness. Avoid all cooking smells at this time, and the ill person should stay out of the cabin even though it looks like a safe haven. Keeping warm is important, and maintaining the fluid level is critical. If eating is possible, crackers, dry cookies, or fruit are best.

Don't hesitate to use some of the commercially available motion-sickness pills, but try them out beforehand. Some cause drowsiness, although there are some available by prescription that have no side effects. To work, they have to be used before the seasickness.

Galley duty is always a chore on a cruising sailboat, but you can simplify it by using paper plates. Since paper plates aren't firm enough to balance on your lap if you dine in the cockpit, or stiff enough for cutting, have a set of conventional plastic plates as well. By putting the paper plate on the solid plate, you have the comoforts of the dining table without dishwashing.

For those items that have to be washed, you can buy a mesh bag and put all the pots and dishes into it. Hung over the stern, the motion of the boat will sluice away most of the food and you'll only have to rinse the items.

There are some tricks to be learned about the icebox or the ice chest that can keep your food cold and fresh. One is to use dry ice in addition to conventional ice. Dry ice will have to be wrapped in paper and shouldn't be touched with the bare hand, but it will keep even a poorly insulated icebox extremely cold. To make it last, don't allow it to sit in water or touch wet ice.

To further aid the icebox in its work, precool everything that goes into it. Before you leave on your trip, store all the icebox foods in your refrigerator overnight, and cool the icebox down with ice cubes at the same time. When restocking during your cruise, make every effort to buy prechilled items so that you won't heat up the icebox. You'll be able to get cold milk and butter, but also buy cold soda and beer, if you can find it.

Use the icebox as little as possible, because every time the lid is opened, cold air will escape. The best method to conserve ice is to use the "hot box" method. Have a second, smaller ice chest with its own ice supply. Every morning, remove the food you'll need from the main icebox and put it in the smaller ice chest. That should include not just the meals, but beer and soft drinks. Make everyone use only the hot box, and save the main icebox for long-term storage.

Check the temperature of the icebox before you depend on it during a cruise. Use an icebox thermometer, and load the icebox with as much food and ice as you plan for your trip. The temperature should hover around 40° for best results.

Keep the icebox as full as possible and it will last longer. The more airspace in the box, the faster the ice will melt. Anything placed directly on ice will also melt it quickly, so be sure to segregate your block of ice and keep cans of food from falling onto it. By the same token, if there isn't a built-in drain, keep the melted ice water from touching the block since it will melt it.

One way to have both ice and drinking water is to freeze plastic jugs of water at home. Stowed in the icebox, they provide cooling until they melt and cold drinking water afterward.

Do as much cooking ahead of time as possible to minimize your galley work. There are a variety of foods that can be precooked, sealed in plastic bags using Seal-A-Meal, and then reheated in boiling water. Don't overlook sandwiches, which can be made ahead of time and then kept fresh and soft in airtight bags, or salads without the dressing.

Milk is always a dangerous food since it can turn bad quickly, but the problem can be solved by using canned milk, which doesn't require refrigeration. There are similar problems with other dairy foods. Cheese should be purchased with a thick rind on all sides and, once cut, butter should be smeared on the cut side to seal and preserve it.

Eggs can be made to last for months by dipping each egg in boiling water for five seconds to seal them. It's a much neater method than the old way of smearing them with wax or grease, and it works just as well.

Don't forget to label all food cans with waterproof marker pens, since the labels may wash off and "mystery" dinners usually aren't very good.

23

~~~~~~~~

Racing

Sooner or later, most sailboat owners get involved in racing to some extent. It usually comes first as a casual "race you back" from the anchorage, but there are all levels of competition that can be explored.

Class racing is feasible when there are enough identical boats that can race together without the benefit of handicaps. In class racing, you'll be governed strictly on the modifications that can be made to your boat and the sails that you can use.

Handicap racing is just that—a way for boats of different sizes and shapes to race together equitably by using various types of handicap systems. For most trailerable sailboats, racing will be confined to either class racing or performance handicap, a loose system based on proven performance of sister boats.

Assuming that you've decided to go all out and chase trophies in the handicap classes, what can you do to your boat to make it faster? There are an endless number of changes and improvements you can make, and you'll have to balance them against your budget and your needs. A spinnaker, for example, is a fairly expensive sail including all the equipment, but you'll need it for most handicap racing. Many classes, however, won't allow spinnakers in their own events, so you'll have to decide whether your use will justify the cost.

Even in strict classes that prohibit anything but the standard equip-

A fleet of trailerable sailboats mixed in with smaller boats prepare for a regatta on an inland lake.

ment on the boat, you can probably "tune up" your stock boat for a little more speed.

The first thing to recognize is that most trailerable sailboats are designed for people who just want to get out on the water. They aren't concerned with efficiency and the manufacturers know this, so they don't make a perfect underwater surface. The keels are the worst point on most retracting boats. If you want a competitive boat, you need to clean up the keel. Don't change the design of it, but smooth it out, fair in the casting blisters, and file off the rough spots. You can use automotive body putty to fill in chips and gouges.

The next thing is to get rid of any extra drag underwater. If your keel retracting cable has protruding bolts, you'll have to figure out a way to eliminate them, especially if you sail in an area where you can pick up seaweed on any protrusions.

Some owners of trailerable sailboats go to great lengths to rid themselves of the drag of the retracting wire. One way to do this is to groove the back edge of the keel and then pull the wire into this groove while sailing to cut the drag and still be able to launch from a trailer.

Another way to smooth the bottom, if you launch by crane, is to block off the keel well with styrofoam to eliminate the turbulence of the open hole.

The stock rudder is probably a plank with the edges rounded. You can reshape it to a foil shape for added speed. Be careful to check the class rules, because some prohibit any such modification.

The last step under water is to smooth off the hull itself. Using 400-grit wet-or-dry sandpaper and then 600 grit sandpaper to finish it, you can lightly sand the entire bottom to rid it of any small imperfections and to smooth out the bottom paint if you have any.

For the class racer, you'll probably be limited to the original working sails or perhaps a larger genoa. But for the handicap racer, you'll want to expand your sail inventory to include at least a spinnaker and the large genoa. With an unlimited budget, you can add many different sails for special conditions: a lightweight genoa for drifting conditions, sails for reaching or running, and so forth.

Interestingly enough, most successful racers of trailerable sailboats have found that they don't need the full array of sails so necessary to bigger boats. The trailerable is more responsive to wind conditions, and one of the most successful competitors has only a spinnaker and a

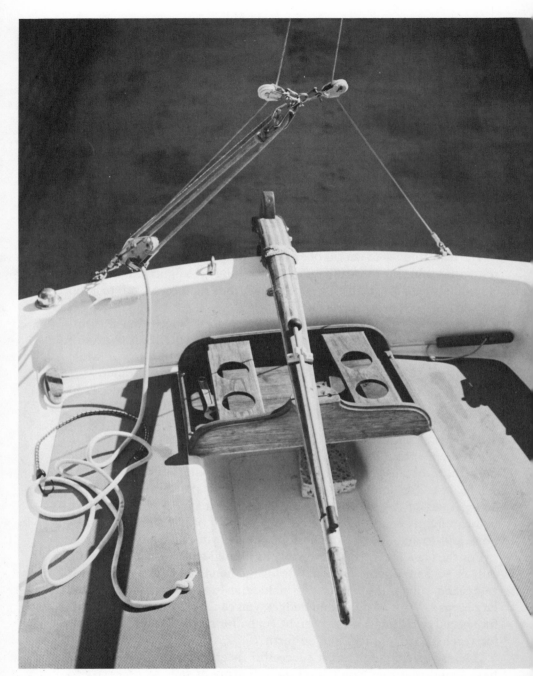

This Venture-21, rigged for handicap racing, has a divided backstay which joins into a single wire above the photo. This allows easy tightening by use of the block-and-tackle arrangement. By pulling down the two blocks on the backstay, the entire rig can be tensioned. By easing off, the headstay can be loosened for running and reaching. The long wand behind the removable tray is used for clearing seaweed off the rudder, and the tiller sports an extension.

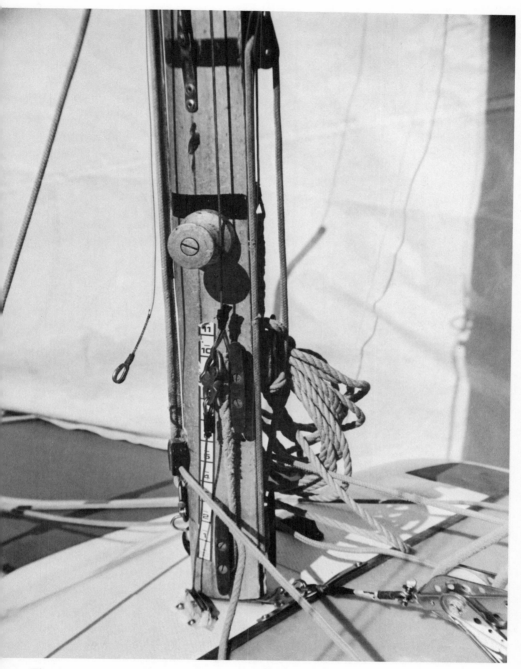

The mast on this same Venture has been fully customized for easy sail handling. The numbers show how tightly the jib has been hoisted, and various halyards and adjustment lines are led through blocks at the base of the mast and then aft to cabin-top cleats.

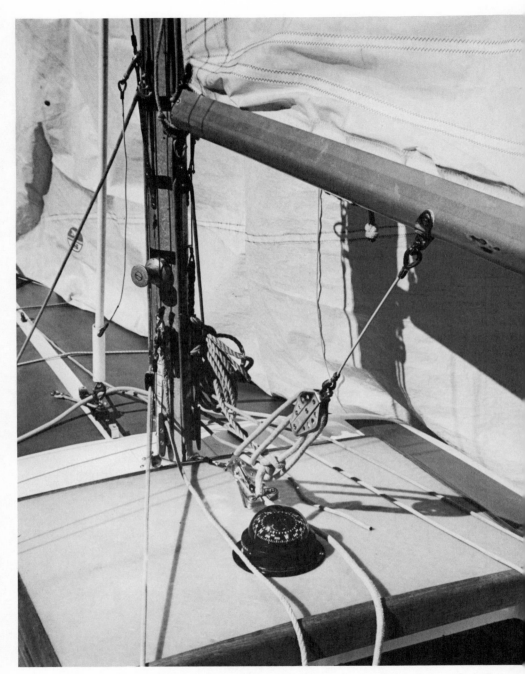

Looking forward at the mast, the husky boom vang is visible. It can also be detached from the base of the mast and moved to the gunwale to hold the boom out in light winds. The hatch-mounted compass is visible to the crew without looking away from the sails.

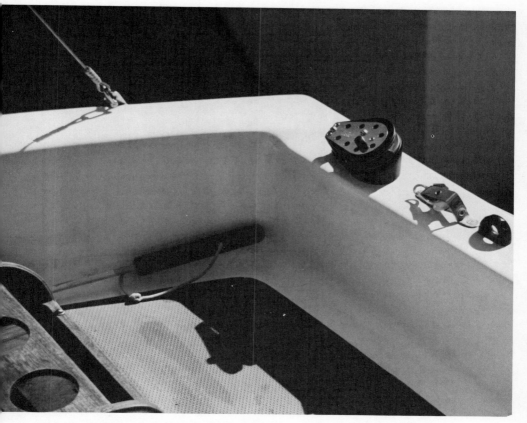

Spinnaker leads are mounted on the aft corner of the cockpit. The ratchet block (farthest aft) is the normal spinnaker sheet, while the two smaller leads are used for light spinnaker sheets and other light sails.

150-percent genoa. He has the ability to reef both the genoa and the mainsail. His plan of action is as follows: in over 14 knots of wind, he reefs the genoa, which reduces the area and flattens the sail slightly. At about 20 knots of wind, he reefs the mainsail. At 25 knots of wind, he changes to the small working jib that was original equipment on the boat. Above 30, he doesn't go out.

Care should be taken about crew weight because the balance is critical. Sending a crewman forward can almost stop the boat and you'll be giving away valuable ground to your competition. It'll take some

This shot of the foredeck shows the "ministay" that runs from the middle lower section of the mast to the center line of the foredeck. It attaches to the roller traveler shown here. The control line leads to the cockpit and allows the crew to control the mast bend and, therefore, the sail shape very accurately.

time before you decide where the crew should sit in normal conditions, but keep crew members grouped in the middle of the boat as much as possible to keep weight out of the ends, which causes hobbyhorsing.

Other areas that need consideration are the mast and its rigging. If the mast is too flexible, you may need to add an additional stay to help it carry racing loads, particularly with a spinnaker.

Larger winches are an aid to the crew, and, if you add a spinnaker, keeping the original small winches as well as the new ones will give you an extra set, which you'll need.

You'll need a good compass for picking up wind shifts as well as

The sheeting angle for the jib, using the track at far right, is about 12°. The "barber hauler" on the track in the center is used to move the jib in to the 7° line for light wind beats. Also shown is the jib cam cleat (empty), which secures the sheet from the opposite side of the boat and thus allows crew members to keep their weight on the windward rail.

This genoa is "all-purpose" since it can be reefed easily. The reefing line starts at the jib tack, runs up the far side of the sail, through the grommet, and then down and back to the cockpit. To use it, the halyard is slacked off, the reefing line pulled tight, and the halyard retightened—a quick process.

This view up the mast shows the extra spreader that supports a diamond stay to stiffen the mast. The short wire just behind the spreader is attached to the main shroud to prevent the center of the mast from moving forward.

simply steering a course. So get one that is readily visible all around the cockpit. The second most important instrument to a trailerable sailboat is a good speedometer. You don't have to go to the expense of buying one that reads to a hundredth of a knot, but the dial should be clearly marked. Because trailerable sailboats are so light, the speedometer will quickly show you when your weight is wrong or if the sails are trimmed incorrectly.

Many trailerable sailboats are delivered with rope halyards. You'll need to change to wire to eliminate the stretch. In addition, you'll need to get the jib up tightly. A small winch is helpful here, although there are other methods using block-and-tackle arrangements.

For the mainsail, you'll need to be able to adjust the outhaul and the downhaul easily. Most boats are delivered with only a piece of line for each corner. You'll want to be able to adjust them when the boom is outboard on a run or reach.

The sailing techniques of racing a trailerable are more appropriate to dinghy racing than to big-boat ocean racing mainly because the boat is light and responsive.

When going to windward, the sea condition is more critical than the wind strength. In a long swell, the trailerable sailboat just bobs over it so it can be sailed fairly close to the wind. When the chop comes up, though, it'll stop light boats. The racing skipper has to make a conscious effort to drive the boat off and keep the speed up in chop. If the wind lightens up and the chop remains, there's not much you can do in a trailerable to prevent the heavier boats from driving past on their inertia.

On a run, the trailerable can often gain considerable distance by "tacking downwind," a technique involving a zigzag course downwind made up of broad reaches where the speed is greater than on a dead run. You'll gain enough speed by reaching to more than make up for the extra distance covered. This is particularly true if you aren't using a spinnaker and your jib won't fill well on a run.

In essence, the keys to racing a trailerable sailboat successfully are to improve the systems that you need, keep the crew weight carefully positioned, and keep the boat speed up, even at the expense of sailing slightly off course.

24

Legal Affairs

If you're buying a new boat, you'll be faced with a multitude of forms, ranging from the receipt for the initial deposit to the purchase order or contract to the financing agreement to a bill of sale and registration papers.

As one lawyer commented, "If you handle every piece of paper as though you were going to have to use it in court, there'll be less time spent in court." The point is, if it isn't written down, don't expect to be able to enforce it. So get it in writing!

From a legal standpoint, each form is equally important and should be given careful scrutiny to see exactly what you are signing. But from a practical standpoint, the most important form is the purchase contract, sometimes called a sales agreement.

The purchase contract should include the amount of deposit paid, a description of the vessel, and the total price to be paid. The vessel description should be full and complete, including the hull number, if the boat is in stock, or a brochure that lists the pertinent facts and equipment. Be sure to list all gear that will be included either as standard equipment or as optional equipment so the builder can't deliver less equipment based on the brochure, which states "specifications subject to change."

Most purchase agreements have extensive fine print on the back, all of which should be carefully scrutinized, preferably by your family attorney. Some clauses that you should add are:

•that the transaction is subject to acceptable financing and insurance and that a marine survey must be completed to the buyer's satisfaction, along with an inspection of all equipment. This allows you to have an independent survey of the boat, new or used, find good financing and insurance, and check over the installation of options on a new boat.

•in the case of a used boat, that the present owner warrants that all electronics and machinery are in operating condition at the time of title transfer.

•that should the inspection not be acceptable, the buyer's deposit will be refunded in full. This puts the pressure on both the new and used boat seller to make sure their product is in good shape.

•that all equipment is to be "installed" or that the boat is "fully outfitted and ready for use." These insure that the outboard has been hooked up and tested, that the sails have been tried, and that all equipment is installed as it should be rather than simply delivered on board the boat.

•a specific delivery date, particularly if you are planning to leave on a trip soon afterward. The dealer often doesn't have full control over the delivery of a new boat or the extra equipment, but this means that you want him to pay full attention to your new boat and not just to shrug it off.

Once you've paid your money and arranged the financing and insurance, you'll need to register the boat. Most dealers can carry this out for you, and you'll be given a certificate of number which must be carried aboard the boat at all times. You'll have to put the registration numbers in letters 3 inches high on both sides of the bow along with the state sticker. If you own the boat outright, the state will send you a certificate of ownership (the pink slip) in a few weeks or, if the boat is financed, it will be sent to the lender.

Your tax bills will be sent to the address on the registration papers, so be sure to keep the address current to avoid paying tax penalties.

You'll also need to register the trailer. This can be handled either by the dealer or the local Department of Motor Vehicles. Attach the temporary paper license plates before you drive with the trailer, and carry the registration in your car.

Warranties may not be important at the time of sale, but they're liable to be crucial later. The key question to ask when signing the papers is: Who is making the warranty—the builder or the dealer? It will be important if one or the other goes out of business and you're left without a warranty or, if the warranty is from the dealer, if you move to another area where you can't get service.

Most printed sales agreements contain a disclaimer that the dealer is making no warranty with respect to the boat and equipment other than those made by the builder, and that there are no implied (unwritten) warranties. On the other side, most states now have laws that force the dealer selling new equipment to warrant that the goods "fit the intended use." Don't count on any warranties unless they're in writing, and then examine them carefully for loopholes.

Your bank will require insurance, and even if you don't finance the boat, you should still provide yourself with adequate coverage. Unfortunately, one of the perils of the sea is marine insurance. There is a great deal to know about the various policies and options. Find a good insurance agent with experience in the marine field. The agent who handles your home and car insurance is probably not competent to recommend marine insurance, so act accordingly.

Your basic insurance is the so-called Hull Insurance, which really covers the entire boat. Most policies are labeled All-Risk Marine Policies, but they aren't. At best, they might be called Almost-All-Risk Policies. They are based on the premise that the only thing that they will cover for loss is an extraordinary event of some sort. The presumption is that when you insure the boat, you are guaranteeing that it is seaworthy. If you do not maintain that condition, your insurance will not cover you. You must also act in a seamanlike manner, since negligence can also void your policy.

Let's look at some examples. If you have allowed the boat to become rundown and have made no effort to keep it in good condition, a dismasting that results from broken rigging (which should have been inspected) will probably not be covered. By the same token, if you launch your boat without putting the drain plug in place and the boat sinks, your negligence does not count as an extraordinary event.

The point is that simply having marine insurance is not enough. You need to maintain the boat and to handle it competently for the insurance to cover you.

The question of value needs to be considered when buying insurance. Many policies for small boats are based on actual cash value (ACV), which means that if the boat is totally destroyed, you will be reimbursed what the boat was worth when you bought it, plus added equipment, of course. That wouldn't be such a bad deal, except that boats are *appreciating* in value, not depreciating. A boat bought five years ago for $10,000 and in good condition is probably worth $12,000 to $14,000, while a new replacement might cost $16,000. An ACV policy will cost you $6,000 to replace your boat!

The alternative is agreed value, where you insure the boat for a set amount and then review it regularly to see if it should be increased to keep up with current market and replacement values. Agreed-value insurance is more expensive, of course, but your agent can show you the differences and in many cases you'll be better off with agreed value.

Most insurance companies that deal heavily in the marine field offer discounts for equipment and skills. A VHF radio-telephone and completion of courses from the Coast Guard Auxiliary or the U.S. Power Squadrons are the two most common, and can result in discounts of as much as 10 percent. Sailboats, in general, have lower rates than powerboats, so beware the agent who doesn't note the difference.

The amount of deductible you purchase is one area where you can earn some real savings. Obviously, the lower the deductible, the higher your premiums. Changing your deductible from $250 to $500 can save more than $100 per year on premiums in some cases. Decide what amount you can reasonably absorb, and then buy the highest deductible you can find. Most of your losses on a trailerable sailboat will be nickel-and-dime items or big bills from damage or theft. Besides, if you have a low deductible and regularly file claims, you're likely to have your rates raised anyway.

One important area that is particularly critical for the trailerable sailboat is to determine a reasonable geographic limitation. Unlike your car insurance, yacht policies usually have a range of 500 miles from homeport, outside of which the policy is void. If you plan to make regular trips to waters outside that range, check the premium for the larger scope. Then check to see how much a separate rider would cost to increase your coverage for each trip. You may find that a year-round addition of distance will cost $100, while riders for each trip will be $25. If you make less than four trips, you're better off with the riders. Just don't forget to notify the agent *before* you leave or you may find yourself uninsured.

If you are buying a new boat, find out about insuring the undelivered boat. There have been many lawsuits over a boat damaged before it reached its owner. Some contracts pass title to the boat at a point when the dealer starts installing extra equipment. In case the dealer goes bankrupt before you've taken delivery but after you've paid for the boat, you may be out the cost of the boat. Check with your agent about this situation.

You'll need Protection and Indemnity (P&I) as well to cover your liability for physical injury to others or damage to their property. A general rule is to buy as much as you can afford, particularly considering today's medical and legal costs. You'll want to cover medical expenses, accidental death, and property repairs with the P&I policy.

For the trailerable sailboat, the Land Transportation policy should be examined. Check with your auto insurance agent to see just what limits are placed on your car policy. Then fill in the gaps. In most cases, the car policy will cover accidents when the boat and trailer are attached to your car, and your car limits will govern the damage payments. But if you've unhooked the trailer while on a trip and it rolls downhill and hits a car, you probably won't be covered on your car policy.

In general, find a good marine insurance agent and then get two more quotes for the same coverage from other agents. Make sure that there are no gaps between your marine coverage and your home (where the boat is stored) and car policies. Review the policy regularly to see if it needs upgrading, and pay the premiums promptly.

SECTION V

Maintenance

25

Hull, Deck, and Interior

Maintenance of the hull and deck is easier than might be expected, although it won't come close to the salesman's promise of a "no maintenance" boat. There is no such animal. Fiberglass comes the closest to being a low-maintenance material, but you'll have to stay ahead of it to prevent some long weekends of work.

You should really start your maintenance campaign before the boat even touches the water for the first time. A good waxing of the hull will prevent scuffs and stains from forming, and it provides a chance to check the entire boat over carefully. Imperfect gel coat is easier to spot when the surface is glossy, and you should bring these spots to the attention of the dealer in the near future.

Every dealer makes an effort to deliver a clean boat, but the reality of installing equipment means that workmen will be tramping back and forth on your decks, leaning ladders against the hull, and leaving metal and wood shavings in all the nooks and crannies. Now is the time to get rid of all the dirt.

Fiberglass gel coat is a remarkably porous material, and it will fade with time unless it is protected from the elements, notably salt water and sunlight. Though many people use automotive waxes on their fiberglass boats, they aren't getting as much protection because the wax is not formulated to fill the pores. Use a good marine paste wax and follow the directions carefully. Some are applied to a damp hull; others require dry application. If that expanse of hull looks endless, use a portable drill with a buffing attachment to do the preliminary polishing once the wax has formed a haze. After that, you can easily touch it up by hand with a clean rag.

The first step is to thoroughly wash the boat, using warm water and a mild liquid detergent that will cut many of the greasy spots and stains. Don't use abrasive powdered cleansers on any smooth surface because they will sand down the glossy surface. You can use the abrasives to clean the nonskid areas on deck, but don't let the cleanser slop onto your smooth fiberglass. A long-handled brush will make cleaning the nonskid easier since it will pick out the dirt in the tiny corrugations. It will also save your back. A sponge with liquid detergent on it can remove spots from the smooth surfaces.

Once you've done the washing, rinse the boat thoroughly to get rid of all traces of detergent and abrasives. If you have persistent oil or creosote stains, try using paint thinner or acetone to remove them.

You'll find that even with exceptional sailing skill and care, you're still going to end up with some minor scratches in the hull or deck. If they don't penetrate the gel coat (no dark spots), you can simply sand them out carefully. Use waterproof sandpaper dipped liberally in water. Start with 200 grit, followed by 320, 400, and 600. This progression will smooth out the scratch, and you can finish up with a rubbing compound and wax.

Most manufacturers or dealers can supply you with gel coat to match your hull colors so you can handle your own patches, but the best advice is to leave everything but tiny nicks to a professional. Gel-coat colors are difficult to match, especially if the boat has faded slightly. And larger damage requires experience to produce a strong repair.

If your boat has been neglected for some time, the gel coat will probably have faded and dulled. The starting point for dull gel coat is a good automotive grade of rubbing compound, applied with a power buffer to save your arms. Once you've done the entire hull, clean off the compound and repeat the process using a good fiberglass wax. In almost every case, you'll find that the color and the gloss have returned.

If the hull is too chipped or dull to respond to patches and buffing, you should consider having it painted. Once you've started with paint, you'll have to maintain it, but there are a number of finishes formulated for fiberglass that will give you years of life. The entire hull will have to be sanded to improve adhesion. The smoothest finishes are sprayed on by professionals. Check with a local boat yard about having your hull painted.

If you leave your boat in the water for extended periods of time, you'll probably need bottom paint. In some fresh-water areas, you'll be able to avoid bottom paint by lightly sanding the unpainted bottom every couple of weeks. But salt water breeds growth, and you can have noticeable growth overnight.

Bottom paint is primarily composed of paint pigment mixed with a poison that kills growth. After eight to twelve months, the poison will have washed out and you'll need to recoat the hull. This will call for sanding the underwater surfaces. You should wear mask and goggles for protection from the toxic dust.

The bottom paint that you choose should be formulated for your area, since each region has different requirements. The easiest application method is to use a large shag paint roller to apply the paint. Use a small paintbrush to touch up hard-to-reach areas, and don't forget to paint inside the keel well. With the keel lowered, you can use a rag dipped in paint and attached to a stick to swab the inside of the trunk with antifouling paint.

The other maintenance operations you'll want to perform on the hull and deck are regular inspections of the swing keel and the rudder. Check the keel cable for fraying or "meat hooks," tiny barbs of wire that indicate a loss of strength. At the first appearance of broken strands, you should change to a fresh cable. Check especially around the swages, since the cable can sometimes bend and then fracture there without being noticeable. Double-check the cotter and clevis pins on the cable to see that they are still secure. Eyeball the pivot pin for wear; it usually indicates wear by starting to leak or "weep" slightly, but don't hesitate to crawl underneath and inspect it with a flashlight.

Check the rudder for fractures if you've run aground before you could release it, and check the tiller assembly for snugness. Crawl inside the stern, check the backing plates for the rudder gudgeons for leaks, bed them again with a silicone sealant, and then retighten the bolts securely. It's a good idea to add a second lock nut to prevent the bolts from loosening while under sail.

Most modern trailerable sailboats have at least some teak trim on deck. This will need some thought if not care. You can do one of four things. The first is the simplest: do nothing. The teak will weather to a grayish shade resembling a New England barn, but it will have no effect on the strength of the wood. Even if you allow it to gray, you can always restore it by cleaning and bleaching, which is your second choice.

There are several teak cleansers and bleaches available, all of which must be applied and then scrubbed vigorously to remove dirt and weathering from the teak. The result will be a light-colored teak just like new, but it will start to weather the minute you finish. Depending on your area and the degree of protection from the elements that your boat receives, it will take weeks or months to reach the gray stage again. To prolong the light coloring, proceed to choice three: oiling the wood.

Oiling the teak serves to preserve the color. You'll recognize the tone as being the same as Scandinavian furniture. The oil will darken with time, so start with the lightest oil you can find and then be prepared to keep after it. Oiling teak is a messy business. It dribbles onto all your freshly waxed fiberglass surfaces, from which it is tough to remove. Nevertheless, oiled teak is lovely to look at. You'll have to re-oil regularly and eventually bleach it all back to bare wood and start from scratch.

The last method of teak preservation is the longest-wearing and the most difficult: varnish. Teak is a naturally oily wood, which means that varnish doesn't adhere to it well. But varnished teak can glow with a lovely radiance. You'll have to sand your bare teak carefully, apply several coats of varnish with sanding between each, and you'll have to add another coat yearly. In time, you'll need to strip off the built-up varnish and start with new layers, but you probably won't keep your boat that long.

The choice of what to do with teak is really a matter of how much work you're willing to do and how much you care what it looks like.

The interior of your boat should receive just as much attention as the exterior when it comes to daily maintenance and year-end sprucing up.

Simply keeping the interior clean is the basic starting point for having a comfortable boat. Spills should be cleaned up immediately before they dribble into an inaccessible part of the bilge, and leaks should be searched out and stopped before they soak the bunks.

In case water does get into the cushions, the best solution is to air them out as soon as possible. Most bunk cushions are foam with a removable cover of either fabric or vinyl. Unzip the cover and remove the foam core. Squeeze all the water out and, if it was salt water, re-wet the area with fresh water to rinse out the salt. When salt water dries, it leaves salt particles, which attract moisture. If a fabric has been salt-soaked and not rinsed thoroughly, it will attract airborne moisture such as condensation or dew, and the result is a fabric that feels clammy even on a dry day.

Sponge off the bunk cover and send it in for dry cleaning at the end of the year to remove all the dirt and grime. The same thing applies to the curtains, which will pick up all the dampness coming in with the air.

If you have carpeting (and you should because bare fiberglass is icy to bare feet in the morning), either use an indoor/outdoor brand that can be hosed off on the dock, or plan to toss the carpet away every year and start fresh. You won't need much, so pick up remnants that can be trimmed easily to fit. Use *lots* of double-sided tape to hold the carpet in place. You don't want to slide around.

If you have vinyl cushions, there are several types of liquid repair kits which can patch small tears or hide cigarette burns.

If you're leaving your boat for the winter, try to arrange for a flow of fresh air through the interior. This can be a cowl vent on deck or screened hatches that are left open. Be sure to keep rain from entering by making hoods for the windows out of cardboard and plastic wrap. Before you close up the boat, prop the bunk cushions up so that air circulates underneath them freely, and leave the drawers open. Always leave the icebox lid open, even if you're only leaving the boat for a week.

If you find that the boat has an overpowering smell of resin when new, you can weaken the scent by wiping down the bulkheads and exposed fiberglass in the cabin with a vinegar-soaked rag. Vinegar also prevents odors and mildew when used to wipe down lockers and in the icebox after you've stored food.

Give special attention to the marine toilet, and don't forget to empty the holding tank before you store the boat or you'll have a real surprise awaiting you. If you flush half a cup of liquid bleach through the head regularly, you'll find that it will stay fresher. The same liquid bleach, mixed half a cup to 40 gallons of water, will sweeten up your boat's fresh-water tank.

The interior woodwork will stay in good condition if you give it reasonable care, which means not scratching it or propping equipment against it while trailering, which will scuff the finish. Before you refinish any interior wood, find out what the factory used. Some mahogany finishes aren't varnish but rather a clear layer of fiberglass resin. Teak is sometimes oiled rather than varnished, so you'll have to determine your starting point before refinishing.

26

~~~~~~~

Spars, Rigging, and Sails

The trailerable-sailboat owner generally takes better care of his mast and rigging than the conventional sailboat owner simply because he raises and lowers it regularly so that he has a chance to inspect and clean if often. But at least once a year, you should schedule a "physical" for your spars and rigging from top to bottom.

Start with the top of the mast and work downward. You should examine all bolts for wear or looseness, and use either lock nuts or double nuts wherever possible. Alternately, you can use one of the various brands of liquid bolt sealant available on the market. Examine the wire and rope halyards for wear, and replace them at the first sign of broken strands on wire or chafe on rope. At the same time, clean and oil the halyard sheaves and check their axles for wear or bending.

Move on to the standing rigging, which, if you've taken care when raising and lowering the mast, should be in good condition. The stiffer wire used for stays and shrouds kinks easily, which then leads to fatigue and breakage. Examine the swage fittings for cracks, and check the wire where it enters the swage—this is a common point for breakage.

Survey the spreaders carefully to see if the mounts are bent or loose. You should have the outer spreader ends taped for sail protection and should remove the tape for inspection at this point. If the stay is wired to the spreader, renew or tighten the wiring and then retape the spreader tip.

All cotter pins, which rely on being bent to hold the clevis pin in place, should be routinely replaced to prevent breakage during the season. While the mast is in a location other than on the boat, run a rag dipped in boat wax up the sail slot or sail track to make hoisting easier.

If you have a bare aluminum spar, wash it thoroughly and use either a mild abrasive or a fine sandpaper to remove the surface corrosion, followed by a good coat of car wax.

If the spar is anodized aluminum, don't sand it. Simply wash it and apply a coat of wax. If the mast is painted, you may want to touch up the chips, using a good two-part epoxy paint intended for aluminum. You should wash and wax the mast in any case.

At the deck level, check the chain plates as thoroughly as possible, although some are hard to see behind the cabin bulkheads. Look for loose bolts or any sign of either corrosion or leakage. You'll want to use a penetrating oil on the turnbuckles to help disassemble them. They should be cleaned and re-oiled.

All winches should be given a once-over, but don't try to disassemble them around the water. The springs can fly a remarkable distance, and they aren't cheap. If you have to remove a winch while afloat, cut a winch-sized hole in the bottom of a cardboard box and place it over the winch. This will keep any stray parts aboard.

Winches build up an accumulation of salt and dirt that should be cleaned out, and the pawls and springs should be re-oiled to the manufacturer's specifications using either light machine oil or a waterproof grease. While you have the drum off the winches, check the mounting bolts for tightness.

Your sails are probably the biggest single investment in your boat aside from the hull, so it pays to treat them with care. Dacron will last five to ten years with reasonable care, and you should devote some of your sailing time each weekend to sail care.

Keeping sails clean is of prime importance, and you should rinse them regularly, particularly when they've been soaked with salt water.

The salt will dry and stiffen the sails, as well as picking up dirt and moisture even when stored. A simple hosing off of the sails when they are hoisted in a light breeze will go a long way toward keeping them in good condition.

Sun, heat, and motion all fatigue the fibers and cause the sailcloth to break down quickly. When you store sails, leave them out of sunlight by either bagging them or using a boom cover for the mainsail. Protect them from heat; storing sails in a car trunk on a sunny day can cut months off the life of a sail. Last, don't leave them up snapping in an afternoon breeze while you have a picnic on the beach. Drop your sails when you're not using them, and don't let them luff unnecessarily.

When you're doing your annual boat clean-up, take the sails off and spread them on the lawn. Beware of doing this on a hot day, though, because you can cook your lawn and leave a large sail-shaped patch of brown grass. Wash the sail thoroughly, using a mild liquid detergent and a soft brush or sponge for spots.

Remove stains with great care since the fabric is a synthetic and doesn't respond well to some fluids. To remove rust stains, soak the affected area in a mild solution of oxalic acid for fifteen to thirty minutes, and then rinse it completely. Start with a weak solution and then move to stronger potions to remove the last traces.

Mildew will often come out with hot, sudsy water, but you can moisten the area with a mixture of lemon juice and salt and allow it to dry. When you rinse the area, the mildew will probably disappear. The synthetic itself can't mildew, by the way, but you can cause mildew to adhere to the surface by stowing your sails wet.

Blood can be removed by forming a thick paste of dry detergent and warm water and letting it stand for twenty minutes before rinsing. Oil and tar are hard to remove, and every effort should be made to avoid them. Scrape off the residue with a knife blade, and then apply dry cleaning fluid to the spot. Under the spot, place a clean rag soaked with the fluid, and gently pat the surface to force the tars through and into the lower pad. This will take time and you probably won't remove the last of the brownish stain, but it will look better.

Once you've cleaned the sail, give it a thorough inspection. Because the stitching in a dacron sail doesn't sink into the fabric but remains on the surface, it is always the stitching that gives first. Inspect the seams carefully; even a few broken threads can cause the whole seam to open like a zipper in a gust of wind. Pay careful attention to seams that chafe against the mast, rigging, spreaders, or life lines. Examine the batten pockets for wear at the inner and outer ends, and check the battens for cracks. The battens should be taped full length so that if they do break, they won't jab through the sail. Examine the head, tack, and clew of the sail where most of the load is carried, and watch for tears around the bolt ropes.

If you find any small tears or broken stitching, drop the sail off at a local sailmaker and have him repair the spots and check the sail over. It'll make your sailing season more pleasant.

27

~·~·~·~·~·~·

Engine

Most of the information you need to properly maintain your outboard is found in the owner's manual. If you don't have one, you should get it from your dealer for the correct model year.

The main problem with most outboards used on trailerable sailboats is that they just don't get used enough. They lie on their side in a damp locker for months, and then they're expected to start on the first pull and deliver full power.

That's not totally unreasonable, but you'll need to inspect and care for your outboard on a regular basis if you expect it to work every time.

To start with, you need to use the proper fuel mixture. Don't pour the oil into an empty tank. Instead, fill the tank one third full with gas, add the oil, shake the tank, and then fill the tank completely. If you plan to store the boat or at least not use the engine for several months, your best bet is to dump the fuel so that it won't turn to a gummy varnish inside the tank.

Inspect the engine at regular intervals for wear and obvious problems. See if the starter cord is beginning to wear out, and watch the spark-plug wires for signs of brittleness or cracks.

When you do use the engine, don't leave it running at idle for long periods. No engine is happy at low speed, and you'll find that the spark plugs will foul with oil and the engine will die when you open the throttle. After you've used the engine in salt water, flush it with fresh water. Modern engines don't need a flushing after every use, but don't leave the salt to work its decay for several weeks either.

You'll probably find that your engine starts faster if you run the fuel system dry at the end of each use. Simply shut off the fuel valve or unplug the fuel hose and let the engine run at a fast idle until it dies. You'll know that there is no more fuel in the system to clog or leak into your bilge.

Once every one hundred hours, you should have the engine tuned and lubed. Since most trailerable sailboats don't use their engine nearly that much in a year, plan to have it done annually.

If you're familiar with engines, you can probably handle the annual tune-up yourself. If not, leave it at an authorized service shop and ask for a spring tune-up.

28

~~~~~~

Trailer

Trailer maintenance should be a regular program rather than a once-a-year check. Along with your regular pretrip inspection, you'll want to perform some regular chores after each use.

Make sure that the tires are inflated to the correct pressure. This is given on the sidewall of the tire. Underinflation can increase tire wear and cause the trailer to sway, while overinflation can damage the boat by increasing the pounding. Buy a good tire gauge; don't trust those at gas stations.

Before launching, let the wheel hubs cool down so they won't suck water in when they are immersed. The hubs can reach temperatures of 180° on the road, and the sudden shock of cold water isn't good for them. The same holds true for your trailer lights. Disconnect them before launching and allow them to cool if you can't unhook them from the trailer.

After each use, particularly in salt water, rinse the trailer thoroughly; be sure to give the brakes and bearings a good flushing with fresh water. Check the brakes regularly for rust or corrosion, and keep them adjusted according to the trailer manufacturer's instructions.

You can't repack your wheel bearings often enough, although most owners only check them twice a season. Be sure to use the proper grease, and don't stint on it.

Ask for a can of touch-up paint when you buy the trailer, and examine the trailer regularly for nicks and scratches. If you touch them up soon after they happen, you won't have to worry about rust. Sand the scratched area lightly and apply a coat of the paint overlapping the good paint on each side.

Check the trailer electrics regularly for light bulbs that may have gone out and for connections that have come loose. Don't allow the trailer wires to dangle below the trailer, where they can be hooked by the road and pull loose.

Check the spare tire often to make sure that it is properly inflated so that it won't be flat when you need it.

Use a light grease on the inside of the trailer hitch to prevent binding on the hitch ball while trailering. Don't forget to grease the trailer rollers regularly or to replace worn carpeting on the trailer pads.

If you plan to keep your boat out of service for several months, you should jack up the trailer to take the load off the tires, which can develop flat spots from all the weight on one side.

Appendix I

Trailer Boat Clubs

Bay Area Balboa Yachts, Box 1405, Palo Alto, CA 94301
Caddo Dixie Cruising Association, 112 Leo Street, Shreveport, LA 71105
Catalina 22 National Association, 20835 Scenic Vista Drive, San Jose, CA 95120
Central California Boaters, 4927 East Leisure, Fresno, CA 93727
Keelhaul Yacht Club, 39 Harbor Hill Drive, Huntington, NY 11743
Land N' Sea Cruising Club, Pacific Marina, Alameda, CA 94501
Mid America Sail and Trail, 4798 Pretty Lake Road, Dousmen, WI 53118
Midwest Cruising Sailors Association, Box 72, Des Moines, IO 50301
North American Sailing Association, Box 3104, Newport Beach, CA 92626
Northwest Outboard Trailer Sailors, 579 Taybin Road NW, Salem, OR 97304
Orange County Boating Club, 2501 Crestwood Street, Orange, CA 92665
San Fernando Valley Sailing Club, 1711 Parkside Avenue, Burbank, CA 91506
Santa Clara Racing Association, Box 83324, San Diego, CA 92138
Trailered Boat Club of Oakland Park, Collins Community Center, 3900 NE Third Avenue, Oakland Park, FL 33334
Tucson Sailing Club, 812 West Camino Desierto, Tucson, AZ 85704
Vagabundos Del Mar, 2415 Mariner Square Drive, Alameda, CA 94501
Venture Owners Association, 2821 North Richmond, Santa Ana, CA 92701
Venture Sailing Club of South Florida, 7001 SW 61st Avenue, Miami, FL 33143
Waukegan Wind Wanderers, 2206 Grand Avenue, Waukegan, IL 60085
Waukesha Cruise Fleet, 4300 Penn Center, Brookfield, WI 53005

Appendix II

Tools

Basic Tool Kit
- Slip-joint pliers
- Standard 8-inch screwdriver
- Phillips 8-inch screwdriver
- Crescent wrench, 8 inch
- Vise-grip pliers
- Spark-plug wrench
- Hammer
- Hacksaw
- Wire cutters
- Plastic toolbox

Additional Useful Tools
- Hand drill and bits
- Files, wood and metal
- Sail palm and needles
- Tape measure
- Swaging tool and Nico sleeves
- Splicing fid
- Socket-wrench set
- Needlenose pliers
- Suction-grip vise

Appendix III

Spare Parts

Engine
  Spark plugs (pregapped)
  Shear and cotter pins
  Water-pump impeller
  Prop nut
  Points and condenser
  Spark-plug wires
  Outboard oil and lubricant
  Service manual

Sail Repair
  Rip-stop tape
  Sail thread, light and heavy
  Battens
  Waxed twine
  Beeswax
  Jib hanks

Miscellaneous
  Dock lines
  Stove rebuild kit with burner
  Light bulbs: cabin, running, compass, instrument
  Fuses
  Flashlight batteries and bulb
  Assorted shackles
  Hose clamps
  Corks
  Toilet rebuild kit
  Cotter and clevis pins
  Electrical tape
  Waterproof tape
  Aerosol lubricant (WD-40 or LPS-1)
  Assorted screws, nuts, bolts
  Tube of epoxy glue
  Silicone sealant
  Sandpaper

Appendix IV

First-Aid Supplies

(To be assembled only with your family doctor)

Phisohex or Betadine antiseptics
Merthiolate
Antibacterial ointment
Burn cream
Vaseline-treated gauze
Adhesive tape
Eye pad
Surgical tape
Absorbent cotton
Gauze bandage
Antiseptic pads
Gauze pads 4″ × 4″
Gauze pads 2″ × 2″
Hydrogen peroxide antiseptic
Adhesive bandage strips, all sizes
Suntan lotion
Sun-screen cream
Decongestant spray
Seasickness pills
Pain-relief tablets
Petroleum jelly

Smelling salts
Scissors
Tweezers
Thermometer
Eye lotion and eye cup
Skin-irritation lotion
Antacid tablets
Laxative tablets
Antidiarrhea medicine
Lip salve
Burn spray
Muscle liniment
Resuscitation tube
Thermometer
Safety pins
Tongue depressor/small splints
Elastic roll bandages
First-aid manual
Plastic first-aid box

Index

Numbers in **boldface** refer to illustrations

Acrilan: boat covers and accessories, 94
advertising, 23, **24,** 61
alcohol stove, 103–5, 106, 161
anchor, 55, 120, 121, 122
   line and chain, 120, 121–22, **122, 149,** 150
   second anchor, 121, 149, 151
   storage, 55, **56,** 148–49, **150,** 151, 165–66, 167
anchoring, 146, 148–51, **149**
   dinghy, use of, 174
   weighing anchor, 151–52
awnings, 94, 96, 174

becalmed, 157, **158,** 159
bell, 120
berths, *see* sleeping accommodations
beverages, 175, 176
bilge, 48, 57, 79, 108, 200
bilge pump, 65, 66, 121, 122, 161
binoculars, 59, 166, 167
boarding ladder or line, 162
boat clubs, 27, 211
boat handling, 13, 30, 146–52
   anchoring and weighing anchor, 146, 148–52, **149**
   boating courses, 27, 192
   docking, 146–48
   sailing singlehanded, 13, 14
   see also navigation; seamanship
boat hook, 121, 148, 161, 163
boating almanacs and handbooks, 171, **172**
boating courses, 27, 192
boating magazines, 23, **24,** 29
boat shows, 25, **25,** 26, **26,** 27
bottom, *see* hull, bottom
broaching, 157

broker, *see* yacht broker
builder, 62–63, 88
   optional equipment, 64–65, 68, 70, 71, 73–74, 75
   problem areas, 60, 77
   reputation, 59–60, 62
   sails, mass purchase of, 93
   trailer, 128, 130
   warranty, 62, 191
bunks, *see* sleeping accommodations
burns, prevention and treatment, 104, 105, 106, 163, 214
buying (trailer), 127–31
buying and selling (boat), 19–88
   advantages of trailerable boat, 11–14, 16
   appreciation of investment and resale, 59–62, 68, 73, 96, 192
   base price, 19, 20
   buying from inventory, 60–61
   closeouts, 60
   deciding kind of boat and cost, 19–22, 76
   discount on demonstrators, 61
   financing, 20, 80, 83, 84, 190
   introductory models, 60
   optional equipment, 61, 64–66, 68, 70–75, 189, 190
   sales agreement/purchase contract, 82, 84, 189–90, 191
   surveyor, 77, 82–88, 93, 190
   used boat, 21, 61, 76–85, 189, 190
   what to look for, 28–63
   see also builder; dealer; yacht broker

cabin, 20, 68
   pop-top, 33, **34**
   see also interior

canvas: boat covers and accessories, 94
car, *see* tow car
carpet, 65, 66, 68, 87–88, 201
Catalina-22, **15**
CB radio, 111, 116–17
charts, 59, 124, 150, 169, 171, **172**
children, sailing with, 36, 71, 120, 174
clevis pins, 199, 204
clothing, storage for, 57, **58**, 59, 166, 167
CNG (compressed natural gas) stoves, 105–6
Coast Guard, *see* U.S. Coast Guard; U.S.
     Coast Guard Auxiliary
cockpit, 20, 30, 37, 43, 45, 68
   awning or sunshade, 94, 96, 174
   cushions, 65, 68, 74
   drains, 43, **44, 45, 46,** 78, 162
   storage area, 121, 149, **150,** 166, 167
   on used boat, 77, 78
   wheel steering, 66, 73
collision, 160–61, 163
commissioning, 65, 68, 86–88
compass, **67,** 124, 171, **182,** 184, 188
construction: boat, 38, 40–43, 45–50, 52, 54, 55;
     see also fiberglass; wood
   trailer, 128
cotter pins, 199, 204
cotton sails, 94
covers: for boat, 94, 96, 137
   for pillows, 167
   for sails, 66, 71, 72, 94, 96, 205
crew, 14, 20
   anchoring, 149, 151–52
   and dinghy capacity, 174
   docking, 147, 148
   and emergencies, 160, 161, 162, 163
   injury, personal, 163–64
   insurance, 193
   launching and retrieving, 143, 144, 145
   leaks, determining, 162
   in light wind, 157, 159
   man overboard, 162
   mooring, 148
   PFDs, 119–20, 121
   racing, **182,** 183–84, **184,** 188
cruising, 14, 173–76
   and optional equipment, 70, 71, 112–13
   sails, 92
   type of boat purchased, 20, 76
   water supply, 108
curtains, 65, 68, 70, 106, 201
cushions, 65, 66, 68, 74–75
   floatable life cushion, 119
   maintenance and repair, 79, 200–201
   of pillows, 167
   V-berth insert, 36, 66, 73, **74**

dacron sails, 94, 204, 205
dampness, 42, 57, 102, 111, 166
   mildew, 79, 94, 96, 201, 205
Danforth, 122
dealer, 23, 25, **26,** 27, 60–61, 62–63, 83
   commissioning, 65, 68, 87–88
   engine, 71, 97
   optional equipment, 64–65, 70, 71, 72, 74,
      115, 190
   registration, 190
   sails, 72, 91
   sales agreement/purchase agreement, 189–
      90, 191
   towing package, 133
   trailer, 128, 130
   used boat, 80
   warranty, 62, 191
deck: color, 68
   fiberglass, **39,** 41, **42,** 43, 78
   hardware, 41, 45–46, **47,** 48, 50, 52, 71, **183,**
      184, 185, 204
   life lines, 46–47, 66, 71
   maintenance and repair, 198, 199–200
   nonskid areas, 65, 68, 198
   pulpit, 66, 71
   on used boat, 78
depth sounder, 48, 78, 111, 114–16, **116,** 150
design, 20, 21–22, 30
   "helm," 29–30, **31**
   interior, 14, 32–33, 35–38
dining area, 32, 36–37, **37**
dinghy, 174
   helicopter evacuation of injured person,
      163–64
   inflatable, 174
   sailing, 174, 188
direction finder, *see* radio direction finder
dismasting, 161, 162–63
distress signaling equipment, 120, 122–23, **123**
docking, 146–48
dock lines, 121, 124, 147, 148
drains: cockpit, 43, **44, 45, 46,** 78, 162
   icebox, 108, **109,** 176
   leaks, 162
   sink, 162
duffel bags, 166
dye markers, 120

electrical system (boat): 49–50, 65, **69,** 70, **107**
   shore power, 66, **72,** 73
   stove, 105
   on used boat, 78
   see also electronics; engine
electrical system (trailer): braking system, 128–
   29, 209

lights, 129, 138, 144, 209, 210
  winch, 130–31, 145
electronics, 111–19
  depth sounder, 48, 78, 111, 114–16, **116,** 150
  maintenance and repair, 111, 118
  radio direction finder, 78, 111, **113,** 113–14
  speed instruments, **67,** 111, 117–18, 188
  on used boat, 78, 190
  warranty, 111
  see also radios
emergencies, 13, 160–64
  distress signaling equipment, 120, 122–23, **123**
  fire extinguishers, 120, 121, 161
  first-aid, 124, 164, 214
  radio, 111, 112–13, 116–17, 161, 163
engine, 26, 30, 71, 97–100, **100, 101,** 102
  for dinghy, 174
  fire extinguisher, 120
  fuel and storage, 98, 128, 167, 207
  maintenance and repair, **101,** 102, 207–8, 213
  mount, 66, 71, 98, **99**
  "sail-drive," **99,** 100
  serial number and identification code, **100,** 102
  as steering if rudder breaks, 163
  storage, 167
  on used boat, 78, 100, **101,** 102, 190
Evinrude engines, 99, 100

fenders, 148
fiberglass, 14, 38, **39, 40,** 40–43, **42,** 45–50 *passim,* 59, 65, 68, 115, 166
  hand lay-up vs. chopper, 38, 40
  maintenance and repair, 13, 40, 96, 197–99
  problems and problem areas, 41–42, 43, 57, 197, 201
  on used boat, 77–78
  water tank, 50, 108
fire, 42, 78, 103, **104,** 105, 161
fire extinguishers, 120, 121, 161
first-aid kit, 124, 164, 214
flags, distress, 120, 123
flares, 120, 122–23, **123**
flashlights, 59, 121, 166
fog, 120, 169, **170**
food, 57, 166, 167, 176
  see also icebox/ice chest
fuel: engine, 98, 128, 167, 207
  stoves: alcohol, 103–5, 106, 161
    gas (CNG and LPG), 105–6
    kerosene, 105

galley, 32, 33, **35, 36, 37,** 50, 103–10, **104, 107**
  food and beverages, 57, 166, 167, 175, 176
  icebox/ice chest, 33, 66, 70, **104,** 106–8, **107, 109,** 167, 175–76, 201
  sink, 33, **35,** 50, 108, 162
  stove, 33, **35,** 66, 73, 103–6, **104, 107,** 120, 121, 161
  utensils and equipment, 55–56, 108–10, 175
  water tank, 50, 108–9, 201
gasoline (for engine), 98, 128, 167, 207
gas stoves, 105–6
genoa (and gear), 66, 70, 92, 165, 179, **186**
  see also sails

halyards, see rigging
hardware, 26, 41, 45–46, **47,** 48, 50, 52, **52, 53, 54,** 71, 78, 79, 115, 162, **183, 184, 185,** 204
  chromed, 65, 68
  engine mount, 66, 71, 98
  layout, convenience of, 30
  maintenance and repair, 46, 199, 203
  pulpit, 66, 71
  on used boat, 78
  see also drains; winches
hatches: closed while towing, 138
  leaks, 33
  screens, 173–74
head, 32, 38, 48, 50, 68, 70, 79, 201
heave-to, 157
heeling, 29, 55, 159
"helm," 29–30
horn, 120
hull: bottom, 179, 199
  bottom, paint, 13, 66, 87, 199
  color, special, 66, 73
  depth sounder, 115, **116**
  fiberglass, 38, 40, 41, 42–43, 77, 78, 115, 166
  hardware and fittings, 48, 52, 115, 162; *see also* hardware
  maintenance and repair, 13, 40, 197–99; *see also* bottom *above*
  overhangs, 30
  registration numbers painted on, 190
  sweating, 42, 166
  on used boat, 77, 78
  wood, 38, 40, 42
  see also deck

icebox/ice chest, 33, 66, 70, **104,** 106–8, **107, 109,** 167, 175–76, 201
  "hot box" method, 175
  maintenance, 107, 201
injury, personal, 163–64
  burns, 104, 105, 106, 163, 214
  cuts, 163, 167

injury *(continued)*
  first-aid kit, 124, 164, 214
  P&I insurance, 193
insects, screens against, 173–74
insurance: personal (Protection and Indemnity), 193
  tow car, 192, 193
insurance (boat), 20, 190, 191–93
  and surveyor, 83, 84
  used boat, 80, 83, 190
interior, 14, 32–33, 34, 35–38, 36, 37, 79
  carpet, 65, 66, 68, 87–88, 201
  curtains, 65, 68, 70, 106, 201
  dining area, 32, 36–37, **37**
  fiberglass, **40**, 42, 48, 49, 65
  head, 32, 38, 48, 50, 68, 70, 79, 201
  light and ventilation, 37–38, 108, 201
    see also ventilation
  maintenance and repair, 13, 200–202
  pop-top cabin, 33, **34**
  storage, **36,** 48–49, 55–59, **104,** 165–67,
    168
  on used boat, 78, 79
  woodwork, 48, 49, **49,** 201–2
  see also cushions; electrical system; galley;
    sleeping accommodations

jib, 66, 70, 72, 92, 165, **181, 185,** 188; *see also*
  genoa; sails
Johnson engines, 99, 100

keel, swing, 14, **15,** 52, 54–55, 179
  maintenance and repair, 54, 179, 199
kerosene stove, 105

ladders: for boat, 162
  for trailer, 130
launching and retrieving, 118, 130–31, **131,**
  140, 143–45
legal affairs and maritime regulations, 189–93
  CB radio, 116–17
  and commissioning, 86, 88
  head, 38, 70, 79
  registration, 190–91
  running lights, 121
  safety equipment, 119–23 *passim*
  sales agreement/purchase contract, 82, 84,
    189–90, 191
  and surveyor, 85
  title clearance and transfer by yacht broker,
    81
  warranties, 62, 71, 86, 111, 191
  see also insurance
life jacket or preserver, *see* PFDs (Personal
  Floatation Devices)

life lines, 46–47, 66, 71
light/lights, 50
  flashlights or spotlight, 59, 121, 166
  natural light, 37–38
  running lights, 121
  SOS, electric, 123
  trailer, 129, 138, 144, 209, 210
  see also electrical system

McGregor, **63**
"Mae West," 119
mainsail, *see* sails
maintenance and repairs, 13, 20, 48, 55, 88,
  145, 197–210
  blood, removal of, 205
  cockpit, 43
  and commissioning, 87–88
  cushions, 79, 200–201
  deck, 198, 199–200
  dinghy, inflatable, 174
  electrical system, 50
  electronics, 111
  engine, **101,** 102, 207–8, 213
  fiberglass, 13, 40, 96, 197–99
  fire extinguishers, 121
  hardware, 46, 199, 203
  head, 201
  hull, 13, 40, 197–99
  icebox/ice chest, 107, 201
  insurance affected by, 191–92
  interior, 13, 200–202
  keel, 54, 179, 199
  mast, 203–4
  mildew, 94, 96, 201, 205
  odors and smells, 79, 105, 106, 108, 173, 174,
    201
    see also ventilation
  rigging, 203–4
  rudder, 199
  sails, 13, 79, 155, 204–6, 213
  spare parts, 213
  speedometer, 118
  stains, 198, 205
  stove, 106
  tools, 57, 130, 166, 212
  trailer, 128, 129, 130, 144, 145, 209–
    10
  used boat, 76, 77, 78, 79, 83
  warranties, 62, 71, 86, 111, 191
  water tank, 50, 108, 201
  winches, 204
  wood, 13, 40, 79, 199–200, 201–2
  see also paint
man overboard, 162
  see also PFDs

mast, 30, 50, **51,** 52, 204
  anodized/painted, 65, 66, 204
  dismasting, 161, 162–63
  maintenance and repair, 203–4
  protection while towing, 138
  racing, **181,** 184, **184, 187**
  radio antenna on, 112
  raising and stepping, **54,** 144, 162
  on used boat, 79
  see also rigging
Midget Ocean Racing Fleet, 29
mildew, prevention and treatment, 79, 94, 96,
    201, 205
  see also ventilation
mooring, 146, 148
motor, *see* engine

navigation, 169, 171
  boating courses, 27, 192
navigational equipment, 124
  almanacs and local guides, 171, **172**
  binoculars, 59, 166, 167
  charts, 59, 124, 150, 169, 171, **172**
  compass, **67,** 124, 171, **182,** 184, 188
  depth sounder, 48, 78, 111, 114–16, **116,** 150
  Light List, 171, **172**
  parallel rules and dividers, 171, **172**
  radio direction finder, 78, 111, **113,** 113–14
  speedometer, **67,** 111, 117–18, 188
  tide tables, and times of sunrise and sunset,
    171, **172**
  watch, 171, **172**
newspaper classified advertising, 23, **24,** 61

oil and tar stains, removal of, 198, 205
optional equipment (boat), 61, 64–66, 68, 70–
    75, 189, 190
  added or installed by self, 65
  on used boat, 77, 80
optional equipment (trailer), 130–31
outboard motor, *see* engine
Owens-Corning Fiberglas, 40

paddle, 124, 163
paint: bottom (antifouling), 13, 66, 87, 199
  hull, 198–99
    special color, 66, 73
  mast, 65, 66, 204
  trailer, 128, 209–10
parallel rules and dividers, 171, **172**
PFDs (Personal Floatation Devices), 119–20,
    121
  and man overboard, 162
  storage, 121, 167
pillows, covers for, 167

portholes, 37–38, 66, 71
  closed while towing, 138
  screens, 173, 174
propane stove, 105
pulpit, 66, 71
pumps: bilge, 65, 66, 121, 122, 161
  salt-water, 108
  sink, 50, 108

racing, 177, **178,** 179, **180–87,** 183–84, 188
  mast and rigging, **180, 181,** 184, **184, 187,**
    188
  Midget Ocean Racing Fleet, 29
  sails, 66, 72, 73, 92–93, 177, 179, **183,** 184,
    184, 185, 186, 188
  type of boat purchased, 20, 76
radio direction finder, 78, 111, **113,** 113–14
  Light List, 171
radios, 26, 78, 113–14
  antennas, 112–13, 114, 117
  CB (citizens band), 111, 116–17
  and emergencies, 111, 112–13, 116–17, 161,
    163
  VHF (very high frequency), 111, 112–13,
    117, 192
registration (boat), 20
  new boat, 190
  used boat, by yacht broker, 81
registration (trailer), 190–91
repair, *see* maintenance and repairs
rigging, 30, 50, **52, 53, 54,** 79, **187**
  broken, 163, 203
  and dismasting, 162–63
  maintenance and repair, 203–4
  protection while towing, 138
  racing, **180, 181,** 184, **184, 187,** 188
  on used boat, 79
  yarn telltales, 159
righting, 29, 55
rub rails, 55, 174
rudder, 52
  broken, 163
  kickup, 52, 66, 70–71
  maintenance and repair, 199
  modifications for racing, 179
running aground, 14, 199

safety, 14, 119–24
  bilge pump, 65, 66, 121, 122, 161
  electric winch, remote-control capability,
    131, 145
  fire, 42, 78, 103, **104,** 105, 120, 121, 161
  first-aid kit, 124, 164, 214
  glass containers avoided, 167
  life lines, 46–47, 66, 71

safety *(continued)*
  nonskid areas, 43, 65, 68
  paddle, 124, 163
  PFDs (Personal Floatation Devices), 119–20, 121, 162, 167
  righting, 29, 55
  signaling equipment, 120, 122–23, **123**
  spare parts, 213
  stove, lighting and installation, 106
  tools, 57, 166, 212
  towing, 129, 138
  underwater openings, plugs for, 48
  vang, 66, 73, **182**
  weather helm, 30
  see also maintenance and repairs; navigational aids
sailing ability (boat), 27, 28–30
sails, 72, 91–94, **95**
  battens, 206
  when becalmed, 159
  with broken rudder, 163
  covers, 66, 71, 72, 94, 96, 205
  custom-made vs. production-line, 93
  and dismasting, 163
  drifter, 92, 93
  genoa (and gear), 66, 70, 92, 165, 179, **186**
  jib, 66, 70, 72, 92, 165, **181, 185,** 188
  mainsail, 72, 92, 153, **154,** 155, 165
    covers, 66, 71, 72, 205
    outhaul and downhaul, 66, 71, 188
  maintenance and repair, 13, 79, 155, 204–6, 213
  racing, 66, 72, 73, 177, 179, **183,** 184, **184, 185, 186,** 188
  reacher, 93, 179
  reefing, 66, 71–72, 92, 153, **154,** 155, **156, 186**
  sailmaker and his reputation, 72, 91–92
  spinnaker (and gear), 66, 73, 92–93, 163, 165, 177, 179, **183,** 184
  staysail, 93
  storage, 165, 167, 205
  used, 79, 84, 85, 93–94, **95**
screens, 173–74
seamanship, 153
  anchoring and weighing anchor, 146, 148–52, **149**
  when becalmed, 157, **158,** 159
  boating courses, 27, 192
  broaching, 157
  collision, 160–61, 163
  dismasting, 161, 162–63
  docking, 146–48
  emergencies, dealing with, 160–64
    see also emergencies

heave-to, 157
insurance affected by negligence, 191–92
man overboard, 162
mooring, 146, 148
rigging broken, 163, 203
rudder broken, 163
running aground, 14, 199
storm conditions, 153, **154,** 155, **156,** 157, 159
surfing, 157
swells, 155, 157
towing, 159
water leaks, determining, 162
seasickness, prevention and treatment, 105, 174–75, 214
seaweed, 118, 179, **180**
self-righting, 29, 55
shore power, 66, **72,** 73
shrouds, *see* rigging
signaling equipment, 120, 122–23, **123**
sink, 33, **35**
  drain, 162
sink pump, 50, 108
sleeping accommodations, 32, 35–36, 37, 68, 75, 174
  V-berth insert, 36, 66, 73, **74**
sounder, *see* depth sounder
Southern Yacht Brokers Association, 81
spare parts, 213
  builder's help in locating, 62
  storage, 57
speedometer, **67,** 111, 117–18, 188
spinnaker (and gear), 66, 73, 92–93, 163, 165, 177, 179, **183,** 184
  see also sails
spreaders, 163, 187, 204
stays, *see* rigging
steering, *see* tiller; wheel
storage (on boat), 55–59, 165–67
  anchor and line, 55, **56,** 148–49, **150,** 151, 165–66, 167
  cabinets, drawers, lockers, racks, **36,** 48–49, 57, 59, 167, **168**
  canvas shoe bag, 167
  for clothing, 57, **58,** 59, 166, 167
  cockpit, 121, 149, **150,** 166, 167
  duffel bags, 166
  engine, 167
  first aid kit, 124, 164, 214
  folding table, 171
  food, 57, 166, 167
  miniature hammocks, 167
  PFDs, 121, 167
  plastic bins, boxes, tubs, 121, 148–49, **150,** 165–66, 167, 212, 214

sails, 165, 167, 205
tools, 57, 166
storage (on land), 12–13, 20, 21, 201, 210
  insurance, 193
storms, dealing with, 153, **154**, 155, **156,** 157,
  159
  see also sails, reefing
stove, 33, **35,** 66, 73, 103–6, **104, 107,** 120, 121,
  161
  gimbaled, 33, 106
surfing, 157
survey/surveyor, 77, 82–88, 93, 190

table, folding, 171
taxes, 190
teak, maintenance of, 199–200, 202
telephone hookups, 117
tide tables, 171
tiller, 73, 199
  extension, **180**
toilet, *see* head
tools: boat, 57, 166, 212
  trailer, 130
tow car (or vehicle), 21, 132–34, 138
  insurance, 192, 193
  modifications, 133–34
  tire chocks for launching and retrieving, 144
  and trailer's braking system, 128–29
towing (on land), 137–40
  backing up, 138, 139–40
  emergency brake chain, 129, 138
  long distances, 137
  passing, 139
  preparing boat, 94, 136, 137, 138, 165
  safety chains, 138
  sway, 136, 139
  turning, 138–39, 140
towing (in water), 124, 159
trailer, 127–31
  braking systems, 128–29, 209
  electric winch, 130–31, 145
  folding ladder for mounting, 130
  lights, 129, 138, 144, 209, 210
  maintenance and repair, 128, 129, 130, 144,
    145, 209–10
  registration, 190–91
  and storage, long-term, 210
  tires, 129–30, 209, 210
  tongue extender, 130, **131**
  tongue weight, 135, 136
  wheel bearings and hubs, 129, 144, 145, 209
trailer hitches, 135–36, 138

U.S. Coast Guard: CB radios monitored,
  116–17

and collision, 161
and safety requirements, 119, 121, 122
severe personal injuries, 163
see also legal affairs and maritime regulations
U.S. Coast Guard Auxiliary: boating courses,
  27, 192
  free boat examination and list, 120–21
U.S. Power Squadrons: boating courses, 27,
  192
upkeep, *see* maintenance and repairs
used boat, 21, 61, 76–85
  engine and electronics, 78, 100, **101,** 102, 190
  insurance, 80, 83, 190
  maintenance and repair, 76, 77, 78, 79, 83
  price, 77, 80, 82, 83, 84
  registration, 81
  sails, 79, 84, 85, 93–94, **95**
  sales agreement/purchase contract, 82, 84,
    189, 190
  surveyor, 77, 82–85, 93, 190
  see also yacht broker
utensils and equipment (for galley and miscellaneous), 55–56, 108–10, 167, 175

vang, 66, 73, **182**
ventilation, 37–38, 173
  cowl vents, 65, 68, 173, 174
  icebox, 201
  and mildew, 79, 94, 96, 201, 205
  stove and cooking odors, 105, 106, 173, 174
  while using boat and sail covers, 96
  wind scoop, 173, 174
  during winter storage, 201
  see also portholes; windows
Venture-21, **180, 181**
Venture 222, **34**
Very pistols, 123, **123**
VHF radio-telephone, 111, 112–13, 117, 192
vinyl-coated boat covers and accessories, 94
vinyl cushions, 66, 74–75, 201
Volvo Penta engine, **99**

warranties, 62, 71, 86, 111, 191
watch, 171, **172**
water: cleaning sails, 204–5
  cushions aired, 200–201
  dampness and mildew, 42, 57, 79, 94, 96,
    102, 111, 166, 201, 205
  for drinking, 50, 108, 176, 201
  leaks, 33, 48, 79, 87, 161–62, 199
  pumps, 50, 108
    bilge, 65, 66, 121, 122, 161
  spray, 94, 169, 171
water tank, 50, 108–9, 201

weather factors: becalmed, 157, **158,** 159
   storms, 153, **154,** 155, **156,** 157, 159
   and suitability of boat type, 21
weather helm, 30, **31**
wheel (steering), 66, 73
whisker pole, 66, 73
whistle, 120
winches, 52, 54, 66, 70, 79, 92
   changes, 66, 73–74
   electric, for trailer, 130–31, 145
   maintenance and repair, 204
   for racing, 184, 188

windows, 37–38, **47,** 47–48, 71
   rain hoods, for storage, 201
wind-direction and wind-speed indicators, 117
wind scoop, 173, 174
windscreen, 33, **34**
wiring, *see* electrical system
wood: hull, 38, 40, 42
   interior, 48, 49, **49,** 59, 167, 201–2
   maintenance and repair, 13, 40, 79, 199–200,
    201–2

yacht broker, 23, 80–82, 84, 190